SPINNER FISHING
FOR TROUT

SPINNER FISHING FOR TROUT

A Proven System of Tackle, Techniques, and Strategies for Catching Trout

Jeff Deitrich

STACKPOLE
BOOKS

Published by
STACKPOLE BOOKS
5067 Ritter Road
Mechanicsburg, PA 17055
www.stackpolebooks.com

Printed in the United States

First edition

10 9 8 7 6 5 4 3 2 1

Cover photograph by the author
Cover design by Caroline Stover
Photographs by the author
Illustrations by Caroline Stover

Library of Congress Cataloging-in-Publication Data

Deitrich, Jeff.
  Spinner fishing for trout / Jeff Deitrich.— 1st ed.
    p. cm.
  ISBN 0-8117-3104-9 (alk. paper)
  1. Trout fishing. 2. Spin fishing. I. Title.
  SH687 .D45 2004
  799.1'757—dc21

                                                    2003011873

To my father, Carl Deitrich, and his fishing buddy Ron Kreidler.

*You two taught me many of these tricks, but most important,
you showed me the adventurous spirit needed to exceed my own lofty goals
in the pursuit of trout fishing. Thanks. (Thanks also for serving as passable
models for many of these photos.)*

Contents

Introduction

Most people think learning how to be a successful fisherman takes years of practice and tons of patience. Much of that comes from the perception that fly fishing is the only way to catch trout and that fly fishing is difficult to learn. I know of more than one college course on fly fishing and fly casting.

The author with a rainbow trout

While all that is great, and I wouldn't want to take anything away from the long hours of practice and fun that fly fishermen certainly enjoy, there is another easier and more productive way if your goal is simply to catch more trout.

Anyone with a modicum of coordination can learn to catch trout on a spinner in *one afternoon*. That statement is correct. I'm not saying that you won't run into difficulties or that patience isn't necessary. I'm not saying that spinner fishing doesn't have its own nuances. But you can catch trout more reliably and more quickly with spinners. And catching trout is what we're all trying to do, right?

Spinner fishing is the most enjoyable thing I know in this world. Nothing can compare to an 8-inch brookie darting out from under a rock to grab the spinner before he sees you; or watching that lunker come out of his lair and feeling his powerful jaws latch on to your line; or—my personal favorite—watching any fish follow the spinner from the deep water of his hole 25 feet away all the way to your feet, where he takes it just before it leaves the water.

It has truly been the joy of my life to this point, and I have spent thousands of hours streamside perfecting (or at least attempting to perfect) my technique. For the most part, the things I've learned are relatively easy, but until you know and practice them, fishing can be less enjoyable than it should be.

There are a thousand other bits of information that I just can't put in a book. You'll have to learn those for yourself as you fish. However, you are welcome to e-mail me regarding any spinner-fishing question you have. My address is jsd102@alumni.psu.edu.

Enjoy the reading. And then go get 'em!

The author on Drake's Creek, Carbon County, Pennsylvania

CHAPTER ONE

Equipment

SPINNERS

Before you can learn anything about spinning, you have to know what a spinner is and how it works. Very simply, a spinner has a blade rotating around a thin metal shaft with a trailing treble hook. The rotating action of the blade is the main attraction, while size, color, and accessories play a vastly smaller role.

The important thing to know about spinners is that almost any brand will work, but you don't want to use anything too flimsy, or it will quickly bend and otherwise get mangled to the point where the blade will no longer spin. You can also make your own spinners at a fraction of the cost of buying them with only a small amount of knowledge, a little time, and the right equipment (ask your local tackle shop for advice if you're interested).

Spinner Size

First let's tackle size. The various brands use the same basic numbering system, with the exception of the CP Swing. A 1 spinner (CP 3) is about $^1/_8$ ounce with a $^3/_4$- to 1-inch blade. This is the standard size for trout streams (although it's a little small for rivers and large streams) and is very effective in most situations. Why?

The lighter the spinner, the harder it is to cast, but the easier it is to retrieve. A lighter spinner does not cast as far as a heavy spinner and is harder to control. At the same time, it does not dive as deeply into a hole as a heavy spinner, so a swift current tends to force the spinner to the surface, where it may bounce across the water rather than spin. If that happens, you have no chance at all to catch a trout. Your spinner must be heavy enough to dive under the current. Usually a size 1 (CP 3) is sufficient, although a size 2 (CP 4) is often needed after heavy rains.

Size 0 spinners (CP 1) are often useful in summertime, when currents are slow and fish are easily spooked. Smaller spinners make less splash and are not as likely to scare the fish. The only problem is you can't cast them as far. Depending on the reel, your distance may be shortened as much as 15 feet from size 1 to size 0. And, as you will read in chapter 8, it is usually more beneficial for you to remain unseen than for the spinner to make a slightly smaller splash. In many situations, you need the extra distance to remain hidden.

Other Spinner Characteristics

Less important is the color of the spinner. I prefer plain silver, but gold, black, and other colors also produce. Though many fishermen will tell you otherwise, there is no proven rule when selecting a color. The most important thing is to keep it shiny. A dull spinner does not attract trout as well. Remember that it's the motion of the revolving blade that attracts the trout, and many times they won't hit it if they can't see it.

Many people like rooster tail spinners, and some like to fit a worm or another natural or synthetic thing on the treble hooks. All these tactics work (obviously, or people wouldn't use them), but to catch the most fish with the least hassle, don't put anything on the end. I've caught more than 7,000 trout in just about 15 years, and almost all of them have come on a plain, metallic-colored, shiny spinner. Trust me. Fish like to hit them.

The last point to make regarding spinners involves the treble hook on the end. I have one thing to say: Keep it sharp. You'd be surprised how many fish you can lose to dull hooks. Carry a sharpener, and use it.

LINE

Most fishermen advise their pupils to choose the lightest line possible for their situation. That's fine for fly fishing or bait fishing. But with spinners, you want to take a step up from the lightest because of the greater wear and tear on your line. If you would choose 2-pound test for flies or minnows, choose 4-pound test for constant spinner use. Why?

Constant spinner use creates line twist and weak spots throughout the line. Therefore, it's best to use heavier line for durability. Too light a line will result in many breaks and tears and ultimately the loss of time and trout. I like 6-pound test with a size 1 spinner because it's very durable and still allows me to cast to a fish too far away to see me. Four-pound test is good for size 0, and you may want to go to 8-pound test for size 2 (and definitely for any larger size).

Any of the name brands will do. Patronize whichever company you like. I have just one caution: Stay away from cofilament lines. They are not as durable as monofilament, though they claim to be. I lost two 18-inchers (one palomino on Bald Eagle Creek in Centre County, Pennsylvania) because of line breakage while fishing cofilament. It was odd because the inner filament broke about $1/8$ inch below the outer filament.

Tying on a Spinner

Next point: How do you attach the line to the spinner? Simply tie it directly to the eyelet. You don't need any leader. However, it is best to use a snap-swivel for even easier attachment. Line can be tied directly to the swivel, and the swivel allows you to quickly change lures, if necessary. More importantly, the swivel eliminates a great deal of line twist. That, in turn, means your casts can go farther, and your line will break less often.

Perhaps the most important advice is to change your line often—about every two weeks with heavy use, or whenever you can see the twists throughout the line. It's also a good idea to frequently cut off the last 6 inches and retie it to the swivel, perhaps as often as three or four times during a day of use. Rocks, tree limbs, and trout teeth all take their toll on those last few inches, so keep an eye peeled and check for signs of fraying at regular intervals. Looping your spinner on a limb, dragging it across a rock, or catching a sharp-toothed rainbow can all cause nicks in your line.

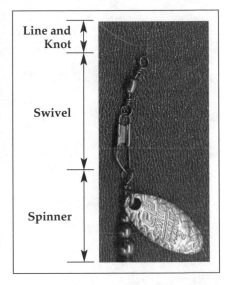

RODS

Don't buy a cheap rod, but there's no need to buy an expensive one either. What do I mean? I mean the performance varies only slightly from rod to rod, so it isn't necessary to buy a tungsten-boron-graphite composite rod with supersensitivity and tough, lunker-resistant action. All that is marketing hype. Those rods are a little better, but are they worth $20, $40, even $300 more? No way. You can get a durable graphite composite rod with excellent sensitivity for $15 to $30. The only caution is, don't go too cheap. Avoid too-good-to-be-true offers, such as two portable rods for $9.99.

My father once bought two telescoping fiberglass rods for $5—and that's what they were worth. They worked great and were very portable,

Brooks Run in Cameron County, Pennsylvania

but the first one lasted only about two weeks before it bent in half right in the middle of playing a nice brookie. I still managed to catch the fish because he was well hooked, but I had to hike back to the car and get my spare rod. The same thing happened to the other telescoper about a week later.

The point is, performance is only slightly better in more expensive rods. Once you get past the cheapest of the cheap, most rods are just as durable.

The simplest way to test a rod—and you can do this in the store—is to attach a reel to simulate the feel when you're fishing, and then waggle the tip back and forth. If it feels stiff and the tip doesn't move much, you probably won't be able to cast very far. If it feels too flimsy, you may have less control of your casts or could even run the risk of breaking the rod.

Generally, fishermen perform this test while holding the rod toward its near end. However, the proper position of your hand while retrieving is forward of the reel. Test it that way, with a reel attached, so that you can feel the balance. Each rod has a long grip section behind the reel (toward the near end) and a smaller grip section forward of the reel. I recommend choosing a rod with the longest available grip area forward of the reel. Your entire hand should be touching the grip section when you're holding the rod in a reeling position. If the grip section is too small, you can lose some control, but more important, you can suffer some uncomfortable skin abrasions or cuts if your hand doesn't fit comfortably in the grip area.

Naturally, I recommend testing the rod on a stream as well. Shop at stores that allow you to return products without a hassle if you're not satisfied (and always save your receipts). The store and the manufacturer should stand behind their products and warranties.

It's a good idea to get a rod with ceramic line guides. Monofilament line wears grooves in metal but not in ceramic. If your metal guides become grooved, they can impede your casting and reeling ability and may even snap off your line.

Some good brands include Zebco and Daiwa in the lower-price category ($15 to $25) and Berkeley and Fenwick in the more expensive range ($30 to $50). Choose whichever material you like. It really doesn't matter. The importance of having a graphite composite or some other kind of ultrasensitive rod is overrated. With spinner fishing, rod sensitivity is not that important. Go with what you feel—not with what the manufacturers and advertisers want you to believe.

Closed-face reel

Open-face reel

REELS

The reel is unquestionably the most important piece of equipment you will buy. Get a good one that you can cast, retrieve, and carry comfortably. If at all possible, tie on a size 1 Mepps and give it a few tosses. Make certain it casts and reels smoothly.

With reels, as with rods, the main difference between expensive and inexpensive is durability. But here it is more important, because if even a minor problem occurs, you may be out of luck for an entire trip. With rods, you can lose an eyelet or a covering somewhere, or your two-piece can become permanently stuck together, and you can still fish productively. But if anything comes off of or gets stuck in a reel, it's finished, so stay away from flimsy plastics. Metal or graphite is a good choice (I favor graphite for rust resistance).

Don't let anyone pressure you into using an open-face reel over a closed-face one, or vice versa. They both work well (I use a closed-face reel exclusively). Zebco and Johnson make perhaps the best closed-face reels, while a good choice for an open-face is Mitchell or Penn (Penn is more expensive). Open- and closed-face reels are mechanically quite different. Open-face reels require you to hold the line with your forefinger as you cast, and to reel with the opposing hand; the reel hangs underneath the rod. Closed-face reels require you to press and hold a thumb release button when casting, and you normally need to switch hands to reel using the same hand you cast with; the reel sits above the rod.

There are also modified closed-face reels with a lever instead of a thumb-release button. These reels are very easy to cast and require you to reel with the opposing hand, as open-face reels do, but they have the internal action of a closed-face reel. This is a comfortable alternative for some anglers.

Typically, an open-face reel provides better balance, because your hand holds the rod at the center of gravity. Open-face reels have an easily interchangeable spool of line, and open-face reel spools have a greater circumference than do closed-face reels, so the line does not develop the tight coiling that can produce tangles. Open-face reels were designed with spinner fishermen in mind and do extremely well on medium and large streams. Their main flaws are apparent on small streams, when many very short casts are required. Consistent casts of less than 10 feet sometimes cause the line to twist and become tangled, often around the reel. Open-face tangles can be quite challenging. The line is sometimes drawn down underneath the spool and wound tightly around the center pin. A pair of tweezers may be necessary to loosen the line.

Open-face reels have what is called a bail—a thin, metal bar that flips from one side of the reel to the other at the end of the cast as the fisherman begins to reel. The bail is spring loaded, but you would be wise to

An early autumn trout on the First Fork of Sinnemahoning Creek in Potter County, Pennsylvania

keep it well oiled and to keep a spare spring on hand, because that is the part that usually fails on an open-face reel. When minor tangles occur, the line sometimes wraps around the bail.

Closed-face reels were actually designed with beginners in mind. Bait fishermen and kids often use these reels, but they are compatible with spin fishing as well. Casting is simplified and more intuitive with closed-face reels. Because you reel with the same hand you cast with, reeling is

The proper casting grip for an open-face reel: Grip the line with the forefinger, and then flip the bail over the front of the reel.

typically more comfortable. Open-face reels often require right-handers to reel with the left hand, which can take some practice to perfect.

Closed-face reels do not present problems with short casts, and they are every bit as accurate as open-face reels, if not more so. However, because they are marketed toward beginners, they are often made of inferior materials compared with open-face reels. This makes them less expensive but also more prone to breakage. Thumb-release buttons are often made of plastic and can fail with constant use.

If you are able to learn how to cast, switch hands, and retrieve with the same hand, closed-face reels are an accurate and inexpensive option, especially if you like small streams. If you occasionally like to fish with bait and have children or other beginners who like to go with you, they are also a good choice. One note of caution: I often see right-handed novices holding the near end of the rod with the left hand while reeling (and testing a rod they are about to purchase this way). Instead, your left hand should hold the rod forward of the reel, near the center of gravity. The near (or butt) end of the rod can be held slightly away from your body or tucked against your waist or midsection for more control.

If you are comfortable retrieving the lure with your off-hand, and if you like a little more reliability and smoothness in your casts and retrieves, you may prefer an open-face reel. They tend to cost a little more but are made of better-quality materials.

In either case, choose a reel with a high gear ratio of 4:1 or better (5:1). This means that each turn of the handle reels in more line and allows you more flexibility in terms of how fast you retrieve your line.

When it comes to a reel, buy quality. But even with that as a condition, you shouldn't spend more than $25 to $40.

BOOTS

Select your boots based on how comfortable they are rather than by brand name or price. As always, try to stay away from the cheapest brands unless you plan to fish only a few times a year. In that case, go ahead and buy your boots from Kmart or another discount store. If you plan on fishing extensively, however, get better quality. I normally buy Northwestern or Gear boots simply because they're inexpensive and usually last about two years (or 400 hours of fishing). I recently found a pair of Gears for $9 at a clearance sale, but you would typically pay closer to $25. And clearance sales are questionable when it comes to cheap boots, because older rubber cracks more easily.

Always try boots on and walk around a bit, just as if you were buying a pair of shoes. Normally, people buy boots about a half size larger than their shoe size so they can wear a pair of thick outdoor socks. The socks provide extra cushioning for walking over rocks and extra warmth for wading in cool water.

Many fishermen like boots with felt soles for extra traction on slippery streambeds. The felt wears out more quickly than the rest of the boot in most cases, so you may have to get a kit to repair them, or take them to an outdoor shop for repair. Boots with felt soles are more expensive, but if you've got the money, they are worth it.

The only other question is, should you buy hip boots or chest waders? If you fish primarily large streams and rivers, and especially if you do most of your fishing early in the year, you probably want chest waders. The extra depth and warmth are worth it. If you fish mostly average and small streams, or if you like to fish late in the season, buy hip boots. They are cheaper, more comfortable, and a lot cooler when the temperature rises. I use hip boots for comfort and mobility, and I do not splurge on them.

Boots should be dried as thoroughly as possible after each use. They often get wet from your own sweat during a day's fishing. For best storage, keep them in a dry place, and don't roll them up or fold them. Folds can cause cracks in any boot material.

VESTS

There are plenty of vest styles and designs available, but only a few things to look for:

- Lots of pockets without loose threads
- Velcro or zipper pockets (I've lost a few things through buttoned pockets)
- A large pocket on the back for carrying an extra sweater, jacket, or raincoat.
- Dark colors—perhaps camouflage—to avoid the wary eyes of trout

Most vests are tan, but many stores now carry darker colors. Tan was and is a good choice for boaters and open waters, because it more closely matches the sky and is less visible to trout. It is also cooler under the hot sun. However, many trout fishermen are under the canopy of trees, and dark colors blend in better there. If you typically fish in sunny spaces, tan is a better choice, but if you're more often under the trees, choose a dark color. This advice applies to clothing in general: Choose the color of your vests, hats, shirts, and even boots to match the background colors of the streams you like to fish.

It's wise to get a vest that fits very loosely so you can wear several sweaters or jackets underneath it. You might want to wear a jacket into the store and try the vest over it before making a purchase.

NETS

The main point here, especially if you do any catch-and-release fishing, is to buy a net made of natural fibers rather than synthetics. Older nylons and synthetics are abrasive and can damage a trout's eyes or gills. A soft mesh material, natural or synthetic, is much better for the fish. Orvis makes a great stretch-and-release net of soft mesh that isn't very deep so trout won't twist themselves in it.

Most fish commissions limit the size of net you can use for trout. Use the maximum size allowable in your state. The trout that require a net are the big ones you'll regret losing, so don't be caught with a net that's too small.

Stay away from cheap plastic handles; the flimsy ones break too easily. Try to buy a net with an elastic string in the handle. This allows you to attach it to the back of your vest so it isn't hanging at your side, which means you can walk through the brush without getting tangled. To avoid this problem, I fish without a net almost exclusively. I take one only when I'm specifically fishing for big trout.

WEATHER GEAR

Raincoat

The most important part of your foul-weather gear is a raincoat or pon-cho—the more formfitting, the better. If you can find one with actual sleeves and a hood that fits tightly over the bill of your cap, buy it. Avoid those one-size-fits-all claims (unless you happen to be that one size that fits snugly into one of those).

Don't just get plastic, get thick plastic. Otherwise, your raincoat will tear on the first decent snag. If you have the money, invest in Gore-Tex or some other type of breathable gear that lets your perspiration out while keeping the rain at bay. These can be pretty expensive, however, well over $100. What you buy depends on what you need to be comfortable and what you can afford. You can wear a $5 piece of plastic or a $250 breath-able rainsuit. I wear a Gore-Tex knockoff jacket that cost about $80.

Gloves

Another helpful item is a pair of gloves, but you need something formfit-ting. If you're wearing loose gloves, you can easily hook yourself. Batting gloves or racquetball gloves work well. There should be leather on the palm and the palm side of the fingers, but the backs can be leather, nylon, or any synthetic; the synthetics are cheaper.

You often have to use your fingers very carefully when tying on a spinner or removing it from a trout's mouth, so fingerless gloves are a great idea. Many sportswear companies make them. I wear a pair of Kenai gloves from Bass Pro Shops, and they are terrific. They were designed for cold-weather fishing and have warm cloth over the back of your hand and a rubber palm, which can be rinsed easily after handling a fish.

If you want to save some money and you know how to sew, you can cut the fingers off an old blue batting glove and hem the finger holes so there are no loose threads. You can usually get away with cutting off only the thumb and the first two fingers. I used to wear an old racquetball glove on my right hand with my left hand bare. I hold trout with my left hand when I remove the hook, and I didn't want to get the trout's protective slime on my glove.

Polarized Sunglasses

Perhaps the most helpful item is a pair of polarized sunglasses. Polarized glasses cut down tremendously on the glare coming off the water, and they also prevent you from hooking yourself in the eye. (Don't scoff; I've often had spinners come hurtling back at me when I jerked them loose from a snag.) One caution is that you shouldn't buy the darkest shades.

You want to cut down on the glare off the water, not the amount of light coming in from above.

Here, too, you can spend a lot of money, but all you really need is a pair of polarized glasses that fit. Polarized sunglasses are not hard to find, and you shouldn't have to pay more than about $10 to $25.

Lucky Hat

Every avid fisherman has a lucky hat. Sometimes it seems like the point is to embarrass your family as much as possible, but as usual, the most important thing is to get one you're comfortable with.

I used to wear a real fishing hat with a sewn-on patch of a Woolly Bugger or something on the front, and it was comfortable. It sat loose on my head but was heavy enough to stay on during wind. I wore it until I was sixteen years old. Then I started to worry about how I looked when we stopped for ice cream on the way home, and I realized that my friends were right when they said it looked stupid. That hat was wearing out anyway, so I switched to a baseball cap. It wasn't quite as comfortable, but it wasn't bad.

Since then, I've switched back to a funny-looking hat because it's more practical. It's a Seattle Sombrero by Outdoor Research—a wide-brimmed, Gore-Tex version of the classy hats you saw in *A River Runs Through It*. Those hats are a lot more expensive, but you have to pay for that kind of style. And you might look more like a fly fisherman, but that's your choice.

Never fish without a hat. Besides protecting you from the sun and the rain, it also keeps off insects, such as ticks. Ticks can carry lyme disease, which is nothing to mess around with. Protect yourself.

MISCELLANEOUS EQUIPMENT

Knives

A Swiss army knife or a Scout knife is great. They're kind of bulky, though, so I sometimes leave my Scout knife in the car and carry a small penknife with a $1^1/_4$-inch blade. It cleans trout nicely and is very compact. When folded, mine is $1^1/_2$ inches long, $^1/_2$ inch wide, and $^1/_4$ inch thick.

License

You'll pay between $20 and $35 for a resident license in most states.

Nail clippers

Besides being handy for clipping damaged fingernails, nail clippers make quick and easy line cutters. Ask at your sporting goods store for a clipper clip that attaches to the outside of your vest so you don't have to keep reaching in your pocket.

Compass
A compass is always a good thing to have when exploring a new stream.

Maps
Always carry a state highway map, at the very least. You can also find detailed U.S. Geological Survey maps at most good libraries, or you can order them. The problem with those maps, however, is that they don't cover a wide enough area. Detailed road maps are available in book form for entire states. The one I use is the *Atlas & Gazetteer* from DeLorme. It also lists interesting sights you might want to visit during your fishing trip.

Write to your state's fish commission for maps. Anything with stream names in your area is helpful.

COSTS
Let's tally up the price tag for outfitting yourself. The accompanying table is broken down into the necessities (as I view them) and accessories. Top-end prices are within reason—believe me, you can go a lot higher if you want to. Bottom-end prices exclude the cheap-

You need a license to fish for trout in every state. While many fishermen wear it on their hat, it is better to find the least visible place on your vest.

Fully outfitted, Scott Golla and the author tackled the South Branch of Tunkhannock Creek in Wyoming County, Pennsylvania.

est of the cheap. If you find the same item for much less, it probably isn't worth anything at all. All prices are regular, not sale, prices. The wise consumer can reduce the low-end cost even more by shopping sales, flea markets, or garage sales or by making some of the items.

Be aware that these costs do not include travel, camping, lodging, and the like. These expenses can be much greater than the equipment itself, but the only one necessary to get yourself streamside is travel.

EQUIPMENT COSTS

NECESSITIES	Item	Low Price	Item	High Price	Item	Good Price
4 Spinners	Hot Tail (@ $1.48 each)	$5.84	Mepps Spinflex Dressed Treble	$21.16	Panther Martin	$9.56
6-lb. line	Super Silver Thread, 300 yds.	$4.99	Berkeley FireLine, 300 yds.	$24.87	Stren Original, 330 yds.	$5.99
1 Rod	Shakespeare Durango	$6.96	G-Loomis GLX Spin	$310.00	Zebco Quantum	$29.99
1 Reel	Zebco 202	$8.96	Shimano Stella	$489.99	Fish Eagle Tournament II	$39.99
Hip Boots	Pro Gear	$14.96	Cabela's Dry-Plus Gold Medal	$189.95	Lacrosse	$29.99
Vest	Pflueger	$14.96	Orvis Pro Guide	$139.95	Crystal River	$19.96
License	PA License w/ $5.50 Trout Stamp	$22.50	PA License w/ $5.50 Trout Stamp	$22.50	PA License w/ $5.50 Trout Stamp	$22.50
Required Total		$79.17		$1,198.42		$157.98

ACCESSORIES	Item	Low Price	Item	High Price	Item	Good Price
Net	Dotline	$4.90	Brodin Classic-Plus Cutthroat	$59.00	Pro Guide Net	$29.99
Hat	John Deere baseball cap, free	0	Outdoor Research Seattle Sombrero	$40.00	Columbia Duck Key	$24.95

EQUIPMENT COSTS (CONTINUED)

ACCESSORIES	Item	Low Price	Item	High Price	Item	Good Price
Gloves	Cut fingers on baseball gloves	0	Fleece-Lined Glaciers	$39.95	Kenai Gloves	$19.99
Sunglasses	Strike King	$6.98	Ocean Waves Shaw Grigsby	$139.95	Cabela's Pro Angler	$8.99
Rain Gear	Ozark Trail PVC Poncho	$5.97	Gore-Tex Guidewear Parka	$219.95	Herter's Hudson-Bay W-P Parka	$59.95
Knife	Ozark Trail Pocket Knife	$1.77	Uncle Henry Rancher	$19.97	Frontier Jack Knife	$4.96
Nail Clippers	Renegade	$2.00	Renegade	$9.00	Renegade	$3.00
Needle-Nose Pliers	Angler's Pliers	$3.99	Pro Series Split Ring Pliers	$18.99	Flat-nose Pliers	$5.95
Compass	Ozark Trail Pin-on	$1.97	Garmin GPS Map 176	$499.00	Deluxe LCD Compass	$49.99
Map	State Road Map	$1.95	Magellan Map 410 w/ GPS	$499.00	DeLorme Atlas & Gazeteer	$19.95
Optional Total		*$29.53*		*$1,045.81*		*$227.72*
TOTAL OUTFIT		**$108.70**		**$2,244.23**		**$385.70**

Prices were recorded on May 18, 2003, at Wal-Mart and Dick's Sporting Goods stores (State College, PA), Cabela's Tackle Shop 2003, and FlyFishersParadise.com catalogs.

CHAPTER TWO

Casting and Retrieving

Casting is perhaps the most difficult aspect of fishing, and it's difficult to describe in a book. Even more difficult, however, is trying to master casting and reeling from a book. It can't be done; you have to get out and practice. And don't waste your time practicing in your backyard if you can be streamside instead. If trout season hasn't opened yet, you can still get out there. Some special-regulations waters are open year-round in most trout fishing states; contact your state fishing agency and ask about them. Practice there. You might actually catch something.

The best places to learn are ponds, lakes, and streams with little or no brush, few trees, and clean bottoms. Especially frustrating when teaching novices is constantly cleaning thick moss from the spinner, because novices inevitably forget to reel right away or don't reel quickly enough.

CASTING

As for spin casting itself, the procedure is extremely simple and is often accomplished by nothing more than a flip of the wrist. Start by reeling in your spinner until it is about 6 inches or a little less from the tip of your rod.

The next step depends on what kind of reel you have. If you have an open-face reel, you grasp the line just in front of the bail with your index finger, and flip the bail to the opposite side. Hold the line firmly against the rod with your index finger. If you have a closed-face reel, simply press the thumb button and hold it in.

At this point, swing the rod tip behind you. The action in your arm should be almost entirely from the elbow out to the wrist. Your upper arm shouldn't move very much at all.

It doesn't matter which direction you use for the backswing. You can swing it forehand, backhand, underhand, or straight overhead, and the

A 10-inch and a 20-inch brown taken on the upper Colorado River in central Colorado

effect will be the same. This makes spin casting very versatile, because you can cast around brush upstream, downstream, and right at your feet from the same position with the same basic motion. Just be careful not to catch your spinner on a tree, bush, or another fisherman.

Before your rod tip has a chance to get all the way back, start your forward motion. This is much the same as the backswing, but it ends with a quick snap of the wrist to get more power into the tip of the rod. In the middle of the snap, release the line from your index finger (or remove your thumb from the button). It takes some practice to know just when to release. If your casts are floating up into the air and landing short, you're releasing too soon. If your casts are smacking into the water not far in front of you, you're releasing too late.

If your casts are shooting straight out at the correct trajectory but you're not getting much distance, chances are you're swinging your arms too much. A fishing rod is not a baseball bat. You must always remember that the power comes from how fast the tip of the rod is moving. It doesn't matter how fast your hand or arm moves if you don't get the proper snap out of your wrist. Practice it—on the stream.

To learn how to cast and retrieve a spinner effectively, you have to get out and practice.

Flip Cast

If you're in tight brush that doesn't allow a backswing, don't worry. Use a flip cast (a type of underhand cast). In a flip cast, you start with a little extra line left out—maybe half a rod's length or slightly more. Then you rock your wrist so the spinner is swinging right in front of you and directly at the target, like a pendulum. When it's swinging far enough that the spinner comes right up underneath your hand on the backswing, do just what you'd do on any other cast—snap your wrist directly toward the hole. This works because the power of a cast is in the wrist, and you can still snap your wrist right in front of you without any mighty backswing.

I urge you to practice a good number of casts just by snapping your wrist as quickly as possible, with no other arm motion. You'll soon see what I mean.

Horizontal versus Vertical

I said before that your backswing could be forehand, backhand, or directly overhead, but in most cases, it's best to make the cast closer to horizontal than to vertical. Why?

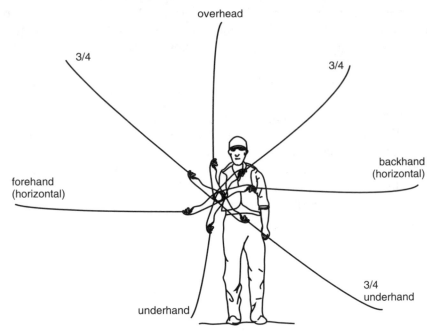

Backswings can be made in virtually any direction. Typically, the backswing and casting motion will be primarily horizontal so that if the timing is off by a split second, the lure will still land in the water. Change the casting motion when there is an impediment, such as low bushes or overhanging trees in front of or behind you.

Timing is tricky in casting, and it's easy to be a little off in your release time. Most often, you'll be casting from a bank to the opposite side of the stream. If you cast in a horizontal motion and release too soon or too late, your spinner will probably still land in the water. If your cast is vertical and you release too soon, your cast will usually find a tree or the opposite bank. That's why you should use a horizontal motion most of the time.

When you have brush on either side, however, and there is only a narrow vertical lane through which to cast, the best choice is a flip cast. An overhead cast is less controllable. You should use a vertical, overhead cast only when there is brush on both sides and at your feet, making all other casts impossible.

Other Expert Casting Tips

A cast isn't complete until the spinner lands. For casts that you feel will be accurate upon release, simply point the rod tip directly at the spot where the spinner should land. Then get ready to reel before the lure lands.

If you see that the spinner is going too far, simply start reeling early. When you reel, the bail of the reel flips, and line is automatically prevented from going out farther. After you've had a little more practice, you might want to try lightly closing your index finger or thumb on the line against the rod to give it more drag. That kind of feather touch can make a cast that was just a few inches long end up perfect.

Another great way to shorten a long cast is to point your rod tip in a different direction. Think about it. If you take two rods and point one rod directly behind you and another directly in front of you, there's a difference of about 11 to 12 feet (on a 5-foot rod) from one rod tip to the other. So, if your cast is going long, just point your rod back the other way. The cast will land shorter by the distance between where your rod tip would normally have been and where it actually was.

You can also alter the direction of your cast by doing the same thing. If your cast is just a bit too far right, point your rod to the left. The force or tension from the line will pull the lure in that direction. It's kind of like throwing a curve ball.

No matter where your spinner lands, *always* be ready to reel immediately. And if your spinner lands *anywhere* in the water, reel it as though it landed perfectly. I've caught numerous trout on bad casts just because I gave them a chance.

> No matter where your spinner lands, always be ready to reel immediately.

In certain cases, especially around logjams and large rocks just above the waterline, you may actually need to cast over a limb or rock to get the lure where you want it. Never fear doing just that. You can retrieve a spinner effectively even when your line lies over a limb.

RETRIEVING

Easily the most important thing about retrieving in spinner fishing is that you have to reel—always and immediately. Actually, that's not always true, but for beginners, it should be. Only on rare occasions do you want the spinner to sink very far—until you've become an expert at getting a spinner unstuck, that is. The treble hooks on spinners can easily attach themselves to rocks, moss, twigs, limbs, leaves, and any other object in the water, such as another fisherman's discarded line. (Please don't discard your line anywhere along a stream and especially not in the water. Coil it around your four fingers, as you would coil a hose, and stuff it deep in your pocket; take it home and put it in the garbage.)

If you're out for the first time, put the spinner in the water in front of you and drag it with about 10 inches of line dangling from the end of your rod. That will give you an idea of what a spinner feels like when its blades are spinning through the water.

You should be ready to reel before your spinner hits the water. As soon as it does, simply begin to reel. Don't jerk the rod toward you at all. Just reel.

Sometimes it's a good idea to make the first two or three cranks of your reel a little quicker than the rest to make sure the blades are spinning, especially in calm water or in very fast water when you're retrieving with the current. After that, all you need to do is reel quickly enough so the blades keep spinning and the spinner stays off the rocks and debris on the bottom.

Some fishermen reel with the rod tip down and some with the rod tip up. It's up to you, and it usually depends on what kind of brush is around and how fast the current is moving. Generally, you should keep the rod tip lower when casting downstream and retrieving upstream against the current, and keep the rod tip higher when casting upstream and retrieving downstream with the current. These actions help keep the spinner low in the water but off the bottom.

> *Never point the tip of your rod at a large fish you've hooked. It's a sure way to snap your line.*

An important point is that you should never point the rod directly at a fish you've hooked, especially a large fish. That's the surest way to snap your line. Keep your line from breaking by keeping the rod pointed away from the fish so that the rod—not the line—absorbs the fish's power.

As you get more experienced (and I mean after a few hours or days, not 10 minutes), you can start to reel the spinner more slowly or let it sink a little bit in deeper water so that it reaches more fish. Most trout lie close to the bottom, and they usually have to come up to strike a spinner, so you want to get it as far down as possible. But don't overdo it. I'd rather miss one trout because my spinner was too high in the water than have to wade in the middle of a hole to get it unstuck and scare every trout around.

Learn how a spinner sinks. Most spinner fishermen view the water as a two-dimensional area consisting of length and width. But streams clearly have depth, and that is often the key. Trout in a deep hole have to rise as much as 10 feet before reaching a spinner. Bear that in mind. Being able to let your spinner sink—but not so far that it gets snagged—is extremely important, especially in higher water conditions.

To practice, cast a spinner into a hole from which you can easily retrieve it, and watch how it sinks. Sometimes it flops lazily like a spoon or like a leaf in the air. Sometimes it shoots to the bottom like a rock. You'll get a feel for how quickly each one goes.

Now, when you're fishing a deep hole and you know the fish are sitting low, cast to a calm spot, and let the lure sink. You'll have to react quickly if you see it sinking fast, or a bit more slowly if it's falling like a leaf. Either way, you want to get it within a foot or so of the bottom before starting your retrieve, which must be done quickly and strongly. The motion of falling in the water often causes the blade to stick and refuse to begin spinning when you retrieve, so a slightly firm, faster beginning to the retrieve often jump-starts it into motion.

Once you become adept at it, you can drop your spinner to deep water over and around rocks and logs and begin a serious effort to reach every fish in the stream.

In any of these scenarios, trout tend to bite in what is known as the strike zone. The strike zone is the area from the middle of the main current to a short distance past the edge of the main current on the side of the stream you're standing on. Or, the strike zone is from 6 inches on the other side of the trout to about 4 feet on your side of the trout.

Although trout will bite outside the strike zone on a regular basis, most trout hit the spinner in this zone. Therefore, you shouldn't reel the spinner at the same speed all the time. It's best to reel fairly quickly until the spinner enters the strike zone, then slow your retrieve, especially if you're turning the retrieve back against the current. This fast-to-slow motion first catches the trout's attention, then allows the trout to catch up to the lure while it is still in deeper water and far away from you. The result, of course, is more trout choosing to hit your lure.

It's often a good idea to stand 10 feet or more back from the bank to avoid scaring trout, especially in low, clear water.

Casting and Retrieving from 10 Feet Back

It's often a good idea to stand 10 feet or more back from the bank to avoid scaring more trout than necessary, especially in low, clear water. This is true for most trout holes in all but the largest streams. Whenever possible, make your first cast (and sometimes many subsequent casts) well before you ever reach the edge of the bank.

> **Make your first cast well before you ever reach the edge of the bank.**

Everything is the same as fishing a hole normally, except that you must cast farther and you must know how to retrieve your spinner when it reaches the edge of the water to avoid getting it caught on the bank. Generally, the technique is to retrieve the spinner normally until it is only 3 to 5 feet from the edge of the stream. At that point, lower the rod tip and point it directly at the spinner. You may need to retrieve line much more quickly as you do this to keep the spinner retrieving normally in the water. Also, extend your arms a bit toward the spinner.

Your goal is to reduce the amount of line between you and the spinner to the absolute minimum.

Now, just as the spinner is about to exit the water, give a quick, short, but firm tug to pop the spinner from the water. If this is done well, you can get the spinner to land at your feet. However, it's better to pull it too hard than too soft, so the spinner often zings back past you. At this point, you can actually control it as a fly fisherman would—allowing the weight of the spinner to carry it back and forth and keeping the line taut until you can control it and bring it to you.

I often zip the spinner past me many times and keep it off the ground (sometimes looping it around me) until I can reel in enough line to bring it directly to my hand. This process does two things: (1) It keeps the spinner from getting snagged too near the fish, and (2) it keeps the line taut, so it can't twist around itself and tangle. Thus, it saves time and doesn't scare fish.

CHAPTER THREE

Where the Trout Are
and Where to Cast for Them

After you've learned the basics of casting and reeling, you get to work and start catching trout. How? You have to know where the trout are going to be and where to cast for them. To me, this chapter is the most important in the book. The following tips should help you consistently catch more trout.

KEEP MOVING

Get up off that stump and start walking. When you are fishing with spinners, you need to keep moving if you want to be successful. The first cast is the most important in any hole, and the next two are also big producers. Beyond the third cast, however, the percentage of strikes drops off dramatically. This means that you're usually wasting your time if you stand around casting into the same hole all day, even if there are trout in it. Trout quickly tire of chasing spinners, so it's best to move on to another trout that hasn't seen your spinner yet. Spinner fishing is not for those who like to take a nap on the bank in midafternoon.

> With spinners, the first cast to a hole is the most important. After the third cast, your chances drop dramatically.

Don't get me wrong. You can have a ton of fun teasing some trout into biting by casting to them for a very long time. If your aim is simply to have fun, by all means do it. In fact, as I note later, you can often tease very large trout into biting by casting to them incessantly. But in general, you're wasting your time if your goal is to catch as many trout as possible.

AVOID COMPETITION

Get away from other fishermen if possible. That includes your fishing companions, especially if they're fishing spinners too. I'm talking about both space and time. If a section of stream hasn't been fished for a while,

These fishermen are standing almost on top of the trout, scaring them for themselves and others. Stay on the bank when possible, and avoid other fishermen.

you want to be the first one to cast for those trout. That often means getting up early to be the first one on the stream. It also means fishing away from the bridges and the sections near the road where everyone else fishes.

If I ever find myself fishing behind another fisherman, especially one using spinners, I usually turn around and fish the other way, or move to another section. Likewise, fishing next to your buddy usually isn't a great idea. My father and I catch most of our fish apart. Typically, I drop him off and then drive upstream about a mile and fish upstream from there. Dad fishes up to the car and then drives the same distance ahead. We almost always meet at the same time. Don't worry. There will be plenty of time for trading stories later. And this way, you're free to exaggerate.

> *You want to be the first person to fish a section of stream that has not been fished for a while.*

FISH THOROUGHLY AND FISH THE COVER

In typical water conditions, trout are found throughout the hole—from the head, through the deep water of the pool, and to the tail. Don't disregard any of these places. To fish a stream thoroughly, you must work each part of the hole. It doesn't take a lot of time to fish thoroughly, however. Usually, only one to three casts are needed for each potential trout lair.

Don't just fish in the open water of the nice holes. Trout are notorious for hiding beneath anything they can find—logs, branches, rocks, bridge abutments, undercut banks, even overhanging limbs. Spinners need to be fished across and along—mostly along—all these places so the trout has to make only one quick motion to grab it before thinking twice.

The accompanying diagrams show a number of stream sections from above. Each diagram shows various obstacles, such as logs, rocks, and trees, plus where the trout will most likely be hiding (though they could be anywhere). Whether in streams with rough, rocky bottoms (top diagrams) or smooth, sandy bottoms (bottom diagrams), trout generally tend to stay low and hide behind any irregularities that slow the speed of the current and create eddies. There is certainly no casting pattern that you need to follow. The important thing to remember is that you should cast at least once into every area that might have trout. If you don't draw out a fish on your first couple of casts, move on.

IF IT AIN'T BROKE AND IF IT IS

If what you're doing is working, keep it up. If it's not working, try something new. Although most of your casts should be made upstream across the current (and your retrieves downstream with the current), try changing your tactics. Cast straight across the current and then cast down the current. Cross the stream and fish from the other side to give the trout a

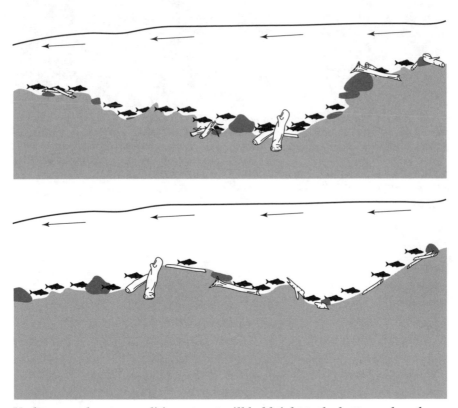

Under normal water conditions, trout will hold tight to the bottom when they are disturbed by trout fishermen. When many other fishermen have been on the water you are fishing, you may need to drag the spinner as close to the bottom as possible so that trout do not have far to move to strike the spinner.

When fishing a stretch of water that no one else has disturbed for some time, expect some trout to be holding near the bottom and others to be out feeding in shallower water and the main current. Seeing you may drive the trout back down to the bottom, which is why most fishermen prefer to remain out of sight when approaching the next hole. Being too visible to the trout is the biggest mistake most fishermen make.

When water levels rise, the water near the surface moves at the highest speed. To avoid swift currents, trout generally move to the bottom (or side, as you will see in subsequent diagrams) where the water moves at the lowest speed. An exception is when temperatures and other conditions set up a good time to feed, in which case trout will move close to faster currents to feed on insects and worms floating by. In high water, trout are less likely to be affected by fishing pressure.

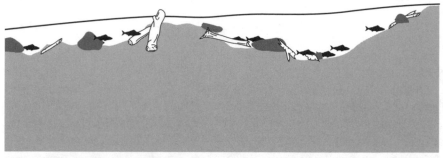

When water levels drop, the stream loses speed. It also loses depth, which makes trout more vulnerable to fishing birds and other predators. Stream temperatures are also prone to rise at such times, especially during warmer months, and the water near the bottom is typically the coldest. Therefore, trout will still seek shelter in the deepest water, although they will occasionally move to shallower water to feed, especially during the cooler morning and nighttime hours. In low water, trout are dramatically affected by fishing pressure and will seek the cover of deep pools, rocks, and limbs at a moment's notice.

At normal water levels, look for occasional trout near shore, though most will be nearer to the main current and deeper water (indicated by circles). In general, trout will stay close to any cover that is available. Fish around the cover and in the deeper pools.

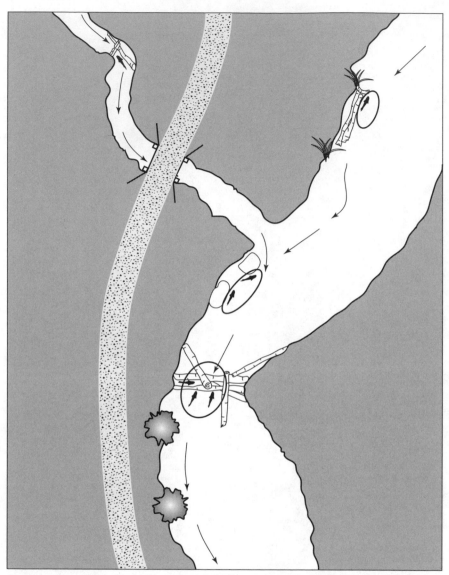

Low water recedes from the sides of the stream, erasing some holes that were there before. Trout are less likely to be found along the shores, except where the deepest water runs against the shore (as with undercut banks and under bridges). In warmer water, trout seek shade, often found under logs, rocks, and bridges, and cooler water, often brought in by tributaries and sometimes underwater springs.

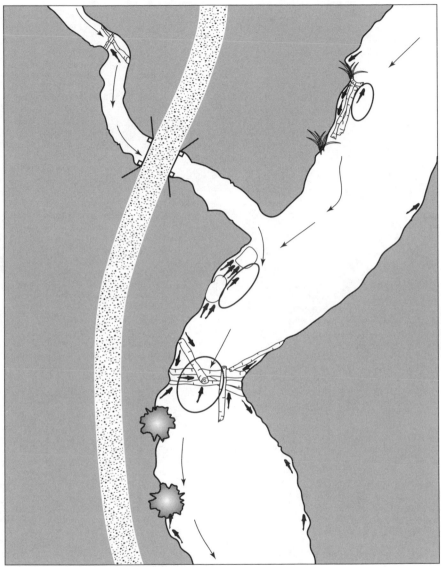

Trout have more options in high water and can often be found in strange places. Note the trout behind the logs in the upper right and to the right side of the logjam at the bottom. In the highest water, it is actually best to fish these backwater areas and any eddies along the side of the stream, which can be quite productive even when the stream is near flood stage. Fishing the heavy current where the holes usually are is often very difficult and nonproductive.

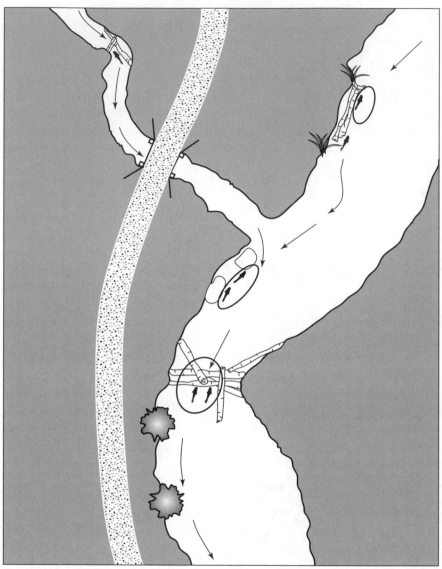

During extremely cold conditions, trout will remain in the deepest holes. The water is warmest close to the earth beneath a thick buffer of water against the cold winter air.

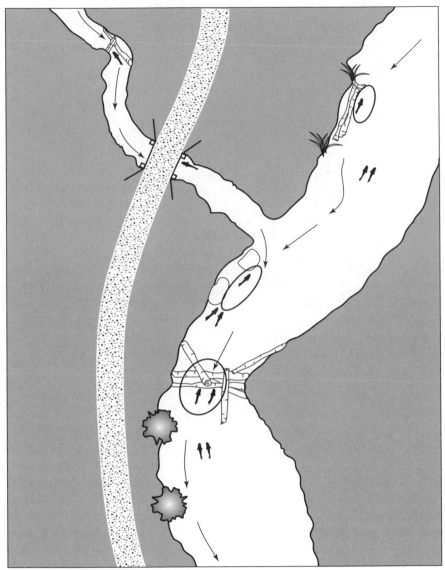

As spawning occurs in the autumn months, trout frequently move away from the main current to shallower water at the tails of pools and the sides of streams. They are often found doing this in pairs. While trout are less likely to bite while spawning, they can be caught. Be wary when moving along a stream, and keep a lookout for trout in these shallow locations. Do not wade where trout are spawning because you could disturb their nests.

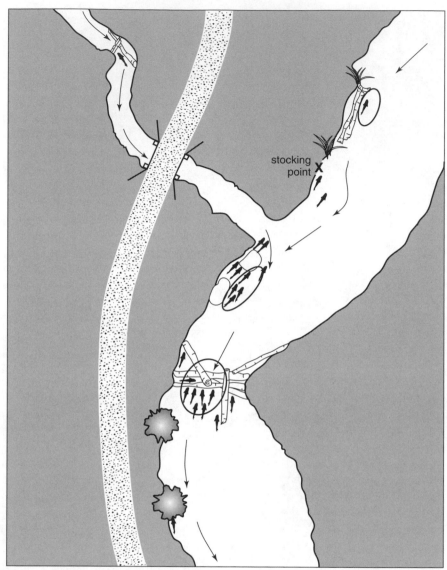

Stocked trout tend to stick in tight packs, the way they were bred in hatcheries. Look for large concentrations in both the deepest and the shallowest water at the insertion point and downstream several holes (depending on the size of the stream). Most fishermen will go for these large concentrations, especially in the well-known holes. However, many biting trout can be found in extremely unusual areas after a stocking. Be careful where you wade, and expect the unexpected. You may find trout in low riffles or shallow side eddies where there is no hole. Trout will also tend to stay on the same side of the stream where they were dumped, especially in high water. When trout are stocked in high water, they are likely to be found in each eddy downstream from and on the same side of the stream as where they were inserted. Find those eddies, and you will likely find trout.

A native brown just released into the golden waters of North St. Vrains Creek in Colorado's Rocky Mountain National Forest

different approach. Retrieve faster or slower, or do both on the same cast, if things aren't going well.

If you have confidence in your technique, let your spinner drop to the bottom for a moment, then snap it into motion quickly. I once enticed a nice 18-inch brown into biting on Mix Run in Cameron County, Pennsylvania, by doing just that. This often works on large trout.

If all else fails, switch to bait or flies or whatever other items you keep in your tackle box. It's rare to fail with spinners, but it does happen. It's been 10 years since I've been shut out, but I know that day will come again.

> **LET'S RECAP:**
> 1. Keep moving.
> 2. Get away from other fishermen and be first.
> 3. Fish the entire hole, not just the deep part.
> 4. Fish along all the rocks, logs, banks, and other cover.
> 5. If it ain't broke, don't fix it. Keep using your spinner and have faith in it.
> 6. If it is broke, try anything to fix it.
> 7. If it can't be fixed, use something else.

SPECIAL TIPS
On Sidestreams and Tributaries

Two places most trout fishermen overlook are sidestreams—where a small part of the stream branches off momentarily before rejoining the main stream—and the first several holes of tributaries to the main stream.

Don't overlook these places, no matter how small they are. Trout can often be found in these two waters, especially stocked trout.

The prime time to look for stocked trout in sidestreams and tributaries is just after the fish are stocked. Sometimes the person stocking the stream accidentally puts the fish in a sidestream. Sometimes that person intentionally stocks them in a sidestream or just up a tributary in order to throw off other anglers. In either case, you can find lots of trout in smaller water. Also, stocked trout are often weak just after they enter the water, as they're becoming acclimated to their new environment. Therefore, the current pushes them downstream. If the trout were stocked upstream from a sidestream—especially one on the same side that the trout were stocked from—they're often washed into the sidestream and may stay there, since smaller water has weaker current. When you know that a stream has been stocked from the left side, pay special attention to the first several holes of the sidestreams you approach on the left side.

> *Never sit and wait for a stocking truck to arrive. Get out and fish! Or at least help them stock.*

You can frequently find stocked or native trout in both sidestreams and tributaries at other times. Tributaries are especially good places to check in the summer months when the main stream gets warm. Tributaries are typically (but not always) cooler, and trout seek out the cooler water. Even sidestreams may provide more shade and cover than the main stream and therefore be slightly cooler for the trout.

Tributaries often drop off rapidly as they approach the main waterway, forming good trout holes. They also frequently pass under roadways and form good pools beneath bridges. Check these places. You'll be surprised more than once.

Getting It Deep

Fishermen often neglect to consider the streambed over which the water flows. The next time you walk along a coulee, pay particular attention to the structure of the streambed. You will note that, except where silt or one solid piece of rock is found, the bottom is extremely uneven. Take a spinner with you, kneel down, and drag it over the contour of the bottom. Think about the size of a 12-inch trout and how easily it can hide alongside a rock right against that streambed.

Now you are thinking three-dimensionally. Too often, trout fishermen think only in two dimensions. They think about how far out and how far to the left or right they have to cast. Once the spinner enters the water, they quit thinking about geometry.

Don't fall into that trap. The depth of your spinner in the water is the third dimension that allows you to reach your quarry. Think about it. If a

This fat rainbow was taken by Ron Kreidler on the South Fork of Beech Creek in Centre County, Pennsylvania.

trout is lying on the bottom of a 12-foot-deep hole and your spinner is 1 foot below the top of the hole, it has to travel 11 feet just to get to the same level. How often is a cast that lands 11 feet from its target acceptable? Not very often. In every case, you want to get your spinner within a foot or so of the trout—often much closer. The cast isn't over, and you don't begin the retrieve, until the spinner has reached the proper depth below the surface.

Trout don't sit near the surface; they usually lie near the bottom—especially large trout. Therefore, you have to be prepared to let your spinner sink in deeper water. This requires delicacy and patience and a lure that is heavy enough to sink through the current.

Generally, you want to begin pulling the lure back when it gets about a foot from the bottom. That gives you a slight margin of error. In clear water, it may be fairly easy to watch the lure drop through the water. In cloudy water, you have to rely on your experience to tell you how fast the lure will drop through the water and how deep the water is likely to be. In deeper water, you need to allow the spinner to sink before retrieving. And when you begin the retrieve, you should

Never disturb another fisherman by walking right next to him or next to the water he's fishing.

start the spinner spinning with a quicker than normal return for the first half second. Sometimes, that half second includes a very short, quick tug. The reason for this is that the spinner's blade may flop out of position as it flutters down through the water. A quick start usually resets it to its normal positon and allows it to spin immediately. Expect hits very quickly when you take the time to let it sink to the bottom.

At times, especially if you know the bed is filled with silt or smooth rocks, you may want to let the spinner drop all the way to the bottom.

This ensures that you get all the depth you can. In fact, you may need that full depth to catch bigger trout. Lunkers often go after food, such as smaller fish and cray-fish, that comes off the bottom rather than from above. They are sometimes attracted to a spinner only after it has come to rest on the bottom for a moment or even a full second. If you're going for big trout, give this tactic a try.

1. Be the first.
2. Don't fish next to others.
3. Keep moving until you find biting trout.

As expected, getting it deep becomes even more important in high water. Not only is the water level up several feet, but the trout also tend to stay deeper in order to stay out of the stronger current near the top. Adding a split-shot sinker or using a heavier spinner is often necessary in high water. Fortunately, bigger trout tend to come out and bite more read-ily in high water, so you can have some of your best days fishing deep when there's a lot of rain.

Of course, getting it deep isn't the only problem. As I said earlier, the stream bottom is like a contour map. Small rocks, large rocks, submerged logs and limbs, and other debris make it lumpy at best. Once you get your spinner down there, you need to retrieve it over and around all these obstacles. Two tactics make this possible to do regularly. First, when fish-ing the bottom, keep the rod tip up—as much as 6 or 7 feet (or more) above the water's surface. If you follow the line from the rod tip to the hooks of the spinner, you'll see that the hooks point up at an angle. When you have the rod tip down, the hooks are also down at a closer angle to the rocks. By keeping that angle up, you decrease the chance that the hooks will catch on the stream bottom.

For the second tactic, your sensitivity comes into play. You need to be prepared at all times to give the spinner a firm twitch if you feel the slightest scraping against the bottom. A quick flick of the wrist is all that is typically needed (which moves your rod tip 6 to 12 inches). That tug both raises the spinner in the water and pulls it through any slight snag. You must be prepared to go deep, and you must not fear losing a spinner, because that's where the fish are. And, as chapter 5 will teach you, there are plenty of ways to loosen that snag and retrieve your spinner.

Stocked Trout versus Native Trout

In the trout fishing world, some people like it easy, and some people like it natural. In other words, a lot of people like to fish for stocked trout, and a lot of people like to fish for native trout. The widely held belief is that stocked trout are easier to catch and that fishing for native trout is more sporting. Of course, it is also true that stocked trout tend to be bigger and meatier than native trout.

Unfortunately, this is too simplistic a view of trout fishing. The reality is that stocked trout are sometimes much more difficult to catch than native trout, and native trout can be extremely easy to catch, especially the smaller they are. And fishing for both can be extremely invigorating and sporting.

In reality, the ease with which a trout can be caught comes down to a simple formula, but it has little to do with whether a trout was born in a hatchery or in the wild. The simple truth is that trout get harder to catch as they face more fishing pressure. Young native trout have not experienced many fishermen or many spinners, so they are very eager to strike them. The same is true of freshly stocked trout. They simply haven't seen any pressure and can be caught in huge numbers over a short period.

Sometimes, however, stocked trout do not acclimate to their new water well and do not bite right away. In fact, sometimes they all but disappear. One day, I was on a tiny mountain brook with water as clear as a bell when a stocking took place. I fished through the half-mile section that had been hit minutes earlier. Although the stream was only several feet wide, extremely shallow, and crystal clear, I spied only one trout as I fished the section thoroughly.

Stocking can also change the action on a stream. Another time, I was having great success through the morning on a nice freestone stream. Then it was stocked, and almost immediately, the fishing died. After catching trout at a rate of about seven per hour, the rate dropped to less

A beautiful rainbow from the Big Quill River on Washington's Olympic Peninsula

The three basic types of trout available in the East are rainbow (top), brown (middle two), and brook (bottom).

than one per hour. In that case, even the native and holdover trout were affected by the stocking.

In addition to occasional acclimation problems, stocked fish see many more trout fishermen in one day than fish in nonstocked streams do. Even on streams that don't see a lot of pressure, it is still extremely rare for freshly stocked trout to see fewer than 10 fishermen a day—and they often see many more. Therefore, not only do they get disturbed by the fishermen, they also see many lures, baits, and flies thrown at them. That kind of pressure often causes trout to stop feeding completely. Their only instinct during such a time is to find cover and survive—not to feed. It is not uncommon to see well over a hundred trout and have trouble catching one. Such a thing is almost impossible on most native trout streams because they rarely face that kind of pressure. Those that do, however, face similar consequences. Disturbed native trout react in much the same way, only faster. Typically, it takes only one or two fishermen to scare off wild trout for a while. Stocked trout are more used to seeing people on a regular basis, and some of them continue to bite on occasion even when fishermen are standing right on top of them. Of course, in the long run, standing on top of them is not wise (nor is it sporting to scare off trout for other fishermen).

All of this relates directly to points one and two in this chapter. As a spinner fisherman, it is your primary goal to fish for trout that have not been fished for by anyone—especially a spinner fisherman—in the longest period of time.

One of the most entertaining aspects of stocked trout is that when they are being pursued heavily by other fishermen and do not wish to bite, some of them can still be caught using expert casting and retrieving skills. They often find cover tight against any available logs, limbs, or rocks and stay as close to the bottom as possible. They won't come out for anything. However, if you can put your lure right in front of them, they may bite.

This takes expert casting, often as close to the far bank and as close to a limb or rock as possible. Often it takes fearless casting that sends the spinner directly into the small openings between rocks, limbs, brush, and the like. It also takes knowledge of how to let the spinner drop in both fast and slow current and how to retrieve it over and around all these barriers while keeping it as close to the bottom as possible.

The technical skill required at these times is at its highest level, and catching extremely large numbers of trout that have already been picked over by many other fishermen is probably the most demanding trout fishing there is. Catching natives is, by comparison, a walk in the park. Native trout typically need a spinner to be cast only within a short distance to attract them. Spooked stocked trout can be had only with exceptional precision.

This is why fishing both stocked and native trout streams is both moral and sporting. Fishing for either is morally acceptable, and the skills required for catching both can be learned by anyone who is open to learning.

If you enjoy fishing for stocked trout, get a stocking schedule from the state fish commission. Although stocking programs vary from state to state, they all offer some kind of schedule to help fishermen with limited time, and it can be an invaluable tool. Plan your outings around the stocking schedule. It would be foolish, for instance, to fish a stream the weekend before it's going to be stocked when the next stream down the road has already been stocked.

Don't sit around waiting for a stocking truck to arrive, however. Even if you know the water hasn't been stocked recently, get out there and fish. Trout streams are never entirely fished out, so try to catch the fish that are still there. I've caught as many as 50 trout on a small stream the day before it was stocked.

SCENARIOS
A Typical Day in May
Let's say it's Saturday morning, about 5 A.M. What should you be doing? Waking up and getting dressed to go fishing, of course.

When the Fish Aren't Biting

Preferably, you'll arrive at your favorite section of a stream that has recently been stocked just as it gets light enough to use a spinner. For the sake of argument, let's say you don't find very many biting trout. Maybe the stream was stocked early in the week and most of the remaining fish are spooked (actually, this happens a lot). After 30 minutes or an hour in that section, you have a pretty good idea that your luck is going to be lousy here. So, what's your next step? Either move to another section of the stream or move to a different stream—one that was also scheduled to be stocked. Then take another hour or so assessing your luck there. The point is that when you're after stocked trout, you have to keep moving until you find a pack of biting fish. That includes moving to another stream, perhaps in another county. Don't waste your time on unwilling fish.

Another thing to remember is that fishermen often will follow other fishermen in the belief that they know where the trout were stocked. Don't make that mistake. You'll catch more trout by getting away from other fishermen. It takes more work to find the trout, but I've enjoyed my best fishing out of sight of others.

And if you want to keep that great hole to yourself, be inconspicuous. Don't let other fishermen know where the trout are. I'm not saying you should lie if someone asks you how you did or where you caught your limit in half an hour, but you don't have to offer every bit of information either.

When You Arrive Second

Let's say you just arrived at your favorite section of stream (during stocking season or not), but somebody has beaten you to it. The fisherman is already testing his line in the first hole. What should you do?

You have three options: (1) Keep on going and fish a different section or a different stream; (2) watch which direction the other person goes and fish the opposite way; (3) if you had your heart set on fishing upstream and it looks like the other person is heading that way, get ready as quickly as possible and walk straight around him.

It's a common courtesy when walking around someone to leave a hole or two between you. Never disturb other fishermen by walking right next to them or next to the water they're fishing. If you want to talk to them, that's fine. But they might not want to talk to you. Say something from a distance first; you'll be able to tell by their reaction if you can approach. That's just common courtesy.

Again, be the first one out there if you can, don't fish next to anyone when you can help it, and keep moving until you find biting trout. These three tactics can't be more important.

CHAPTER FOUR

The Strike, the Play, and the Catch

Your cast is made perfectly, you begin retrieving properly, and the stage is set. What can you expect from the trout? Basically, you can expect one of three things: nothing, a follow, or a strike (or sometimes several strikes by more than one trout).

NOTHING

Nothing is pretty easy to explain. The trout doesn't want your spinner. Unfortunately, there are two versions of nothing: One is when you can't see the trout, and the other is when the water is clear and you know the trout is there.

If you can't see the trout lying there and it doesn't come out to look at your spinner, you may as well move on. The only reason to stay would be if you knew for sure that there were fish in that stretch of water. In that case, you could move, cast again, or change your cast and retrieve. Usually, you'll want to make another three or four casts, and you should change your cast and retrieve each time.

Don't stay too long casting for one stubborn trout, however. Remember, you're trying to catch trout, period. You're not trying to catch that one particular trout. So move on to the ones that are biting.

I'm not saying it isn't fun to try to outwit an especially obstinate trout, but without some sign that it's interested, there's no reason to continue fishing for it—unless, of course, that trout is exceptionally large. Then you might want to stay and throw everything you have at it.

THE FOLLOW

The trout may follow your spinner or at least make a motion toward it. To me, this is the most thrilling part of trout fishing with spinners. It's something that just isn't the same in fly fishing, bait fishing, and rarely in

A nice rainbow fooled by a spinner

minnow fishing. I've had trout follow within an inch of my spinner for 40 yards from the middle of a deep pool all the way to the shallow water a rod's length in front of me.

Imagine the thrill of a fly fisherman when he gets a trout to bolt toward a fly and come crashing through the surface as he tries to set the hook at just the right moment. Impressive, isn't it? Now imagine that same trout, but this time, instead of grabbing your offering out where your cast lands, it follows the lure all the way back to your feet. It could accelerate and grab the lure at any time, and you hold your breath and keep your reel as motionless as possible to avoid scaring the trout. The excitement is long-lasting, and the thrill is there whether the fish strikes or not (of course, it's stronger when it strikes).

Admittedly, the vast majority of trout don't follow the spinner in to your feet, but many trout follow the spinner for quite a few feet before turning back or striking. The rule here is to keep casting until the trout stops following or until you catch it.

Sometimes a trout will follow the spinner repeatedly without ever striking. And I know of one stream a short drive north of Penn State University where virtually all the trout follow the spinner—but they follow up to 15 feet behind the darn thing. I don't know what's in the water to make them do that, but you can bet it's the most frustrating stream I know.

About 20 percent of the time, a trout will continue to follow a spinner after the first strike.

You can decide when you get tired of casting for that one trout without success, but I wouldn't waste much time.

Remember, we want biting trout. You're most likely to catch a trout on your first three casts, and the same is true of follows; trout are most likely to follow a spinner on the first three casts.

THE STRIKE

When a trout strikes your spinner, it either gets hooked or not. The first reaction in either case should be a very short, firm tug to try to set the hook. Why short? There are two reasons. First, when a trout strikes a spinner, it rarely takes the spinner deep in its mouth. In fact, many times the trout just bumps the back of the spinner. When that happens and the trout doesn't get hooked, it usually turns around and heads back. But about 20 percent of the time, the trout comes after the spinner again and follows it for several more feet. So you don't want to give a huge tug that the fish can see or that jerks the spinner from the water with a splash, or you'll certainly scare the trout back to the hole.

Sometimes, the trout hits your spinner two, three, even four or five times on the same cast. Sometimes that's one too many, and you catch it. And that's the goal, right? Imagine your excitement when that trout hits and misses your lure two or three times and comes back for more! It sometimes takes a great deal of patience to land a trout on a spinner, but when you do, that feeling of pride and accomplishment can't be beaten.

The second reason to keep your tug short is that the trout that do get hooked are often barely hooked. If you give a hard, long tug instead of a short, firm one, you can easily tear the bit of skin holding on to your spinner. I can't tell you how often I've landed a trout just as it fell off the hook or taken a hook off a paper clip–thin piece of skin on the fish's mouth, but it happens a lot. So remember, give a short, firm tug.

When a trout is still striking, you should keep casting to it.

If you miss the trout, try again, even if you hooked it for a bit. Many biting trout strike a spinner on several casts in a row. In fact, I've had some trout strike my spinner on nearly two dozen casts before I caught them or they got bored. I caught one of my largest trout on about the sixtieth cast (a mile or so upstream from the Ohio River on Mill Creek in Beaver County, Pennsylvania); it was a 22-inch rainbow. About twenty or more of those casts produced strikes. The rule here is that when a trout is still striking, you should still be casting to it.

Once you have the fish on the line, it's simple: Reel it in. That means hold the trout firmly with no slack in the line. Reel the trout in when it's not providing too much resistance. Some novices reel frantically and don't stop. Doing so could pull the spinner loose. A firm but delicate grip is best when reeling in a trout.

A brown trout took my dad's spinner on a misty Young Woman's Creek in Clinton County, Pennsylvania.

Remember, don't point your rod tip at the trout, especially a large one. Most trout don't put up enough of a fight to drag out the line the way they tell it in most fish stories. A 12- or 13-inch trout shouldn't drag out any line if you're fishing 6-pound test. If it does, you have your drag set too light.

This brown from Colorado's Big Thompson River rested in the shallows before I removed the spinner.

Your drag is there to give line when the trout pulls hard enough to damage or break it. You can test your drag by pulling on the line right out of the spool. If it won't budge, loosen the drag. If it comes out fairly easily, tighten it. Losing a big one, or having a 10-incher drag your lure through a hole where there was a big one you didn't want to scare, will make you wise pretty quickly. But save yourself the heartbreak and take my advice: Test the drag first.

THE PLAY AND THE CATCH (OR CATCH-AND-RELEASE)

As far as playing the trout goes, what you do depends on whether you plan to keep the fish. When you're planing to catch-and-release—and I urge you to do so (if you're using the spinner correctly, you should have to play a lot of catch-and-release)—you should be playing the fish more quickly. You don't want to exhaust the fish so completely that it can't recover.

When releasing a trout, it's best to remove the hook without taking the fish fully out of the water. I've seen some people bounce them across a dusty roadbed and then toss them back in. I doubt that those trout survived.

You should also wet your hands before holding a trout. Don't squeeze too tightly, and keep your fingers away from the eyes and gill covers as much as possible. If you plan on returning a fish, never put your fingers into its gills to get a grip. If you have to rip the gills or the tongue, or if you draw much blood, you should keep the fish. Damaging the gills is probably the worst thing you can do to a fish short of squeezing its innards out.

Once the trout is off the hook, gently lay it back in the water. Some fish need a minute or so of coaxing before they're strong enough, so you might want to hold it upright in the current and gently swish it back and forth to give it more oxygen. If the fish still wants to turn on its belly after a minute or two, you should keep it.

To cut down on the damage to the trout, it's a good idea (and in some places it's required) to fish with barbless hooks or with the barbs bent down. Carry a few of these spinners with you for those frequent times when you catch more than your limit. Another great item to have along is needle-nose pliers. They make removing hooks a breeze in most cases, and they keep your fingers from being cut by the spinner and by the trout's tiny but sharp teeth.

A 21-inch rainbow from Manada Creek in Lebanon County, Pennsylvania

If you plan on keeping the trout, you can care for it any way you want. Make sure you have something to carry it in and some ice to pack it in during a warm day or a long trip.

Some fishermen like to gut their catch immediately. I've also seen some fishermen club trout to death as soon as they land them (I assume it's meant to be a humane way to get the death over quickly). Others wait until they get home to gut their catch. I think it's best to do it on the stream, when possible, because it's quick and easy to clean up. However, many western states have problems with whirling disease, and, where this is the case, it may be illegal to dispose of fish entrails in the stream. Be sure you know your state's regulations. If you cannot dress your catch on the stream, use a sealable plastic bag to contain the fish waste until you can dispose of it properly. Many states require that you leave the head on the trout while you are streamside for purposes of identification.

My friend Kenny Hong and his first trout from Harvey's Creek in Wyoming County, Pennsylvania

I'm in favor of catch-and-release fishing and lower creel limits. These practices keep our trout populations at attractive levels and make the fishing better for all of us. Most important, this cuts down on the huge harvests registered on the day of a trout stocking. Keep only the fish you plan to eat, and think about surprising your friends or relatives with some fresh, cleaned trout. They'll be very thankful.

CHAPTER FIVE

Tangles, Snags, and Knots

Tangles and snags are two of the biggest problems for novices, but there are ways to deal with them. The first way, of course, is to avoid them in the first place.

TANGLES

Tangles are usually caused by line twist, as if you held the line between your finger and thumb and rolled it. These twists eventually cause the line to wrap around itself. Once that happens, there's no simple way to undo the tangle, so it's wise to try to prevent line twist. A few tips follow.

- Soak a new spool of line in warm tap water before you spool it onto your reel (it's also a good idea to soak a spool in warm water before you head out for the day).
- When spooling new line, lay the new pack of line on its side on the floor. Tie a firm knot onto the reel (see the knots section) and trim off the excess. Hold the incoming line between your thumb and forefinger so there's no slack line coming onto the reel. Stop reeling when $3/8$ inch is left from the top of the reel; otherwise, the line can slip off the spool.
- Avoid reeling directly against the current, which causes more line twist. Even when you're retrieving the lure upstream, it's best to retrieve at an angle to the main current.
- Allow the spinner to spin out occasionally. After you pull the spinner from the water, dangle it in front of you until the line untwists on its own.
- Always be on the lookout for extensive line twist, and change your line frequently (at least once a week during heavy spinner fishing).
- If worst comes to worst and you can't untangle it, keep an extra reel or extra spool in your car.

No matter how hard you try to avoid it, you will eventually get a tangle. It's impossible to prevent entirely. Once it happens, you need old-fashioned patience, a good set of eyes, and often a pair of nail clippers to cut off the tangled line.

> *Try every technique to remove a snagged spinner before wading in.*

If you're attempting to untangle the line, never pull it taut. That will simply tighten any knot that may exist. Another good idea is to carry a pair of tweezers. Sometimes you can use them to get a good hold of a piece of line.

SNAGS

A snag happens when your spinner or line gets caught on some object (sometimes on your own spinner, line, rod, or even yourself). Again, it's best to prevent snags altogether. Some tips follow.

> *When retrieving a snagged spinner, don't pull hard immediately.*

- Before casting, be aware of where your backswing will go, and make sure there aren't any bushes or tree limbs (or people) to snag.
- Never cast to a spot you can't see.
- Before you cast, make certain that you're not overlooking a small branch in your casting zone or a submerged log or rock that isn't readily visible.
- If your cast is not accurate, cut off the line flow and pull it back toward you before it lands. Be ready to reel quickly.
- Reel quickly enough so your spinner never touches the bottom.
- Don't reel your spinner too close to logs, rocks, moss, or other debris in the water.
- When walking through brush (or anywhere), cup the lure in the palm of your hand and keep the line taut. Better yet, reel the spinner in to the tip of your rod and learn to carry it through the brush that way (discussed in more detail later).
- Despite all these cautions, *be fearless*. Don't avoid casting to a tough place because you're afraid of getting caught. You can usually get unsnagged.

The single most important thing in retrieving a snagged spinner is what you do the moment you feel the snag. *Do not pull hard.* Give a very light tug to see if it's really snagged. If it is, decide how best to get it out *before* giving a Ruthian yank.

There are several different kinds of snags and a variety of good tactics for getting out of them. I recommend that you try every technique from where you're standing before you wade in. You can often remove a snag without disturbing the water or the trout.

Bottom Snags

Moss, Grass, and Other Vegetation. These are the easiest snags to get out of. All you need is a long, strong pull. Keep the pressure on until it gives way.

Rocks. Rocks are often easy to get loose from. First, let the line go completely slack, and then give a short tug. Repeat this several times. If that doesn't work, simply walk to the other side of the rock (sometimes by crossing the stream) and tug in the opposite direction. The spinner usually comes right off. If you can't walk to the other side of the rock, you might be able to get your line on the other side. I often use the current to drag some slack beyond the rock. When you get a substantial amount of slack on the other side, lower your rod tip so all the line is on the water, then snap it back quickly. This often works. I've even gone so far as to tie some slack line onto a stick or small rock and throw it to the other side to get that pull from the opposite direction.

Logs and Limbs. Limbs are usually easy. A series of quick, firm tugs usually frees your spinner. But if one or more of the hooks are embedded in the wood, you have to go in and get it. The same goes for logs. If the hook is in the wood, it's unlikely you can pull it out just by jerking the rod. You have to go in and actually grab the spinner with your hand. An exception to this rule is if the hook is stuck in bark. The older the tree, the looser the bark, and several hard tugs often pull the bark right off the tree, along with your spinner.

> *The worst thing you can do when you cast into a tree or bush is to try to yank it back before the spinner comes to rest.*

If the spinner is stuck underwater, you don't always have to get wet, however. A great trick is to reel in all the line until your rod enters the water and the spinner is tight against the rod tip. Then try to push the spinner back out the way it went in. This works about 80 percent of the time, so it's worth trying before getting wet.

Bank Snags

As with bottom snags, you usually have to go get your spinner when the hooks stick in a log or limb on the opposite bank. If the hooks are not embedded, however, a very quick, firm jiggling of the wrist often creates enough slack to pop the spinner off. The idea is to get the rod tip moving back and forth very quickly. Just keep jiggling for 10 to 15 seconds, especially if you can see the spinner flopping back and forth. This works about two-thirds of the time.

Tree Snags

The worst thing to do when you see your line zinging into a tree or over a limb is to try to yank it back before the spinner comes to rest. This can cause the line to wrap around the limb many times, and you'll probably have to go get it or cut it off. Instead, when your line enters the tree or bush, gently and quickly close your finger on the line to keep more from going out. Then wait until the spinner comes to rest.

If the spinner itself is stuck, you can usually get it out with a quick jerk or with the jiggling motion used for bank snags. If the line is stuck and the spinner is dangling on the other side, the following trick works 95 percent of the time: First, wait until the spinner has stopped swinging back and forth and is fairly still. Reel the line in until the spinner is within an inch of the spot where the line is caught. Do this very slowly and carefully to avoid looping the spinner up into the snag. Then give a sharp, quick tug with your wrist.

If the line is dangling over just one thin limb or twig, you should get it out 99 percent of the time. In fact, you can usually turn it into a nice cast by reeling the spinner right up to the twig and then giving a sharp, quick tug (if you're making a cast out of it, just make the tug a little less sharp and quick). That usually pops the spinner over the twig, and it lands about a foot on your side, where you can reel it back in as though it were any other cast.

> Always take your discarded line with you and dispose of it properly.

Clothing Snags

If your spinner gets stuck on your clothing, don't pull hard until you examine it. If the barb on the hook is not through the material, just be careful and delicate. The hook will come right out. If the barb has gone through the material, the clothing can still be saved with little damage. Carefully pull the hook toward the barb firmly but without undoing the weave of the cloth. A slight stretch of the material is what you want. This often makes the entry hole large enough to loosen the hook by pushing it away from the barb as you attempt to remove it.

Flesh Snags

The same principle applies with body parts as with clothing. If the barb is not engaged, removing the hook takes just a delicate moment. If the barb is engaged, loosening the barb takes a painful moment. Sometimes a knife or clippers is helpful to remove hardened skin or to provide a clean cut rather than a ragged one, which would result if the hook were ripped out.

If the hook happens to go all the way through and come out the other side, the best approach is to push the hook through far enough so that the barb is entirely through the flesh. Then take a pair of wire cutters and clip off the barb. That should allow you to pull the remainder of the hook through easily. If you are unable to do this, or if the hook is caught somewhere delicate, such as near your eye, visit the nearest emergency room as soon as possible.

Snags on Your Own Line

Occasionally, you'll catch the spinner on your own line. This typically happens in three ways: (1) as you're swinging the spinner on a backcast during a flip cast; (2) when you reel the spinner up close to the rod tip in preparation for a cast or for walking; and (3) when you're pulling the spinner from the water back toward you (usually when it's snapped back at a high speed).

In the first case, the snag is simple. It usually occurs between the reel and the first eyelet of the rod, and only one hook loops around the line. The problem is that this typically happens when your bail is open or your button is pushed. If you let go with your other hand to free the snag, the line may come out of the reel without any tension on it. That, in turn, can cause line twist and create a tangle. So, what do you do? As always, remain calm. Keep the line taut from the reel, and use your off hand to grab the line where it comes out of the reel. Point the rod tip up at a steep angle to allow the spinner to drop down toward your hand. Move your off hand so that it pulls the line back out the way it went in, and you're free.

In the second case, the spinner usually catches the line between the last two eyelets near the rod tip. If you wish to get it off without stopping and using both hands, give out a little slack so that the spinner hangs down 4 to 6 inches between those two eyelets. Then jiggle your rod so that the lure bounces up a few inches. Typically, just a few jiggles coax the lure off the line. Sometimes, though, the line has looped around the end of the rod once before the spinner catches on it. You can use the same technique, but it's successful only about a third of the time instead of more than three-quarters of the time. You usually need to stop and use two hands if the line has looped around the rod.

The third case happens most frequently when you miss a trout as you're trying to set the hook too firmly, or when you're trying to loosen your lure from a snag in or near the water. Pulling hard causes the lure to shoot right back toward the rod, and sometimes it catches the line or comes back between the line in the guides and the rod. It also has a lot of slack, so line twist may cause a significant tangle. Again, be cool, and don't make any unneccessary movements, which will only make tangles worse. Instead, stop and examine the problem and then determine a course of action. One of the techniques described above will work.

Snags on the Rod

These are typically simple snags in which one or two hooks loop over the rod, often out near the tip. They can be taken care of with one flip—not even a jiggle. Use your wrist to give one small flip upward and then another short flip downward and toward the spinner (away from the barb and open space of the hook). It might take two or three flips, but the hook almost always comes off.

Sometimes the line and spinner wrap around the rod. As long as the spinner is not snagged on anything and is hanging free, you can simply start the lure swinging back the other way with a twirl of your wrist. This will eventually unwrap all the line.

Snags of the Spinner Itself

These snags are often very curious. In one case, the spinner simply folds backward one spinner length and actually catches the last inch of line before it connects to the spinner. A quick series of jiggles almost always takes care of this problem. In other cases, however, it looks as though the spinner has caught the line; however, it is possible for one of the hooks to actually go through the eyehole of the spinner itself where the line is tied to it (or through the eyeholes of the swivel). In these cases, it's very rare to get unsnagged by jiggling or other methods. You normally need to stop and use two hands.

Other Snags

The worst thing to get snagged on is the debris left behind by people. This can include discarded fishing line, boots, shoes, tires, burlap, plastic bags, all types of fences, and so on. Most of these materials have less give than natural stream snags, and you're often forced to wade in and retrieve your lure by hand. That often includes using a knife to cut through the debris. These hazards are some of the most frustrating. Please don't add to anyone's grief by discarding such items in the water, and always take your discarded line with you to dispose of properly.

TRANSPORTING YOUR SPINNER TO AVOID SNAGS

How you walk with your spinner is a matter of preference, but I recommend that you reel the spinner up tight to the rod tip. When you do it, the spinner is sticking straight out from the end of the rod, but the hooks are facing back toward you. This is an advantage when walking forward through almost all brush, because the open side of the hook is facing the wrong way to get caught. I move through most brush without a worry. Of course, you must always pay attention to the rod tip as you walk, because if it does get caught, it can snap off if you let it get bent backward at too severe an angle.

Some people recommend holding the spinner in your hand or dangling it a few inches from the end of the rod. Doing the latter means that it often gets caught on the rod or the line at the end of the rod. Holding it in your hand is risky, because if your line gets caught on something, it can be pulled taut, yanking the spinner into your skin. If you do hold the spinner in your hand, try to hold the line just above the spinner, and don't pull the line completely taut. This gives you a split second to react in case you do get caught on something and avoid a nasty puncture wound.

When you put the spinner in your vehicle, it's best to attach it to the eyelet closest to the reel and pull the line taut. Never leave the spinner near the end of the rod, and never leave the line slack. Those are two easy ways to catch the spinner on the interior fabric of your vehicle or on any other gear you have inside. The same is true when you arrive home. You might also consider—especially if you have young children—taking the spinner off of the swivel and storing it in your vest or tackle box. Better to be safe than sorry.

KNOTS

In spinner fishing, knots are not complicated. At most, you need to know only three types of knots: one to connect the spinner or swivel to the line, one to connect the line to the spool of the reel; and one to connect the ends of two different lines. In fact, many spinner fishermen know only one knot. Talk about ease of preparation; it's much different than people spending thirty minutes on their truck beds before they are ready to hit the stream.

Open-face reels have a removable spool. Most tackle shops will spool the line for you at little or no charge, so you never have to learn how to tie the line fast to the spool or how to tie two ends of lines together. When you want to change line, just pop the old spool off and put it in your vest, and pop the new spool into place. This way, you only need to learn how to tie the spinner or swivel to the end of the line, and all that requires is knowing how to tie your shoes using a simple knot. Note that virtually every knot you tie will be slightly improved if you dampen the line just a bit as you pull the knot tight.

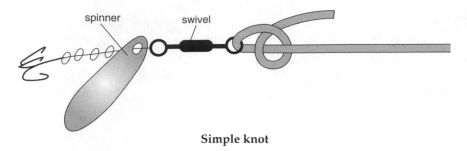

Simple knot

To tie a simple knot, run the end of the line through the eyehole of the spinner or swivel and lay the end back against the line in the opposite direction. Leave 2 to 4 inches from the eyehole to the end of the line. Fold the end back around the incoming line, and stick the end through the hole between the incoming and outgoing lines (between both lines and the eyehole). Pull it tight. Repeat four more times. With a pair of clippers, cut the end of the line to about $^1/_8$ to $^1/_4$ inch from the knot. Firm up the knot by holding it between your thumb and index finger and giving a steady, one-second pull on the line.

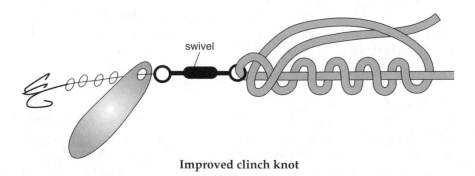

Improved clinch knot

Although the simple knot works just fine, is easy to learn, and is quick to do, some fishermen prefer a stronger knot. The improved clinch knot is an excellent choice. To make an improved clinch knot, run the end of the line through the eyehole of the spinner or swivel, and lay the end back against the line in the opposite direction. Leave 4 to 5 inches from the eyehole to the end of the line. Twist the end around the line about five times (you can do this by rolling it in your fingers, or you can do it with two hands). Then, leaving the end of the line slack, put the end through the first gap next to the eyehole, leaving a loop open as you do so. Next, run the end through that loop. Pull on the end to tighten the coils. Then pull the main line tight and trim as described above.

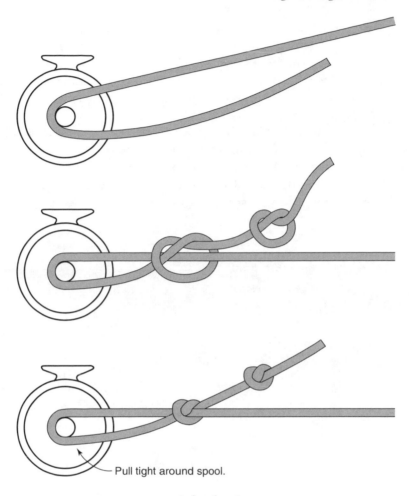

Arbor knot

Fishermen who use closed-face reels must learn two additional knots if they want to get serious about trout fishing. Although these reels come spooled with line initially, there is no removable spool, so to change the line, you need to tie an end directly to the spool after unspooling all the used line. You can use just two loops of the simple knot described above to do this, in which case you need a pair of slender scissors to reach in and trim the end close to the knot. Or, you can learn to tie a form of noose called an arbor knot, which you can then slip around the spool and tighten afterward.

To make an arbor knot, loop the end of the line around the spool and leave about 10 inches between the spool and the end. Cross the end over the main line, then loop it back around the main line and run the end through the loop. Leave about 4 inches from the knot to the end, and pull the knot taut but not tight. Take the end and loop it back around itself only once, then run the end through the loop. Make this knot close to the first one, perhaps only ¼ inch away. Tighten this second, smaller knot, and clip the end close. Then pull on the main line, which will draw the first knot tight to the spool.

Typically, you should do this at least once per season. However, unspooling and spooling an entire reel of line is time-consuming and expensive. You can usually get away with unspooling 50 to 75 yards at a time and then tying the end of the new line directly to the end of the remaining old line still on the spool. To do this, use a double uni knot.

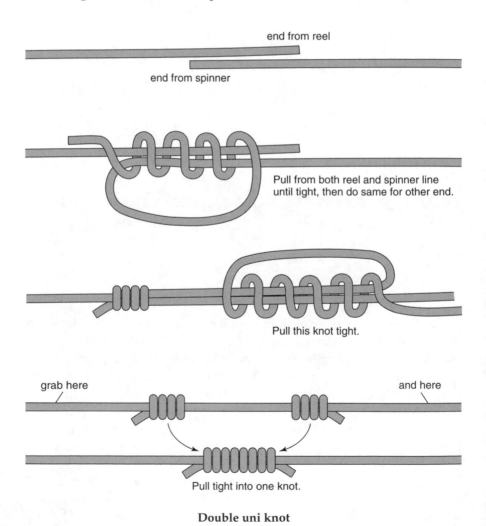

Double uni knot

To tie a double uni knot, lay the two ends facing each other. Pull one of the ends about 8 to 10 inches past the other end. The two lines should still be parallel at this point. Take either end and loop it less than halfway back to the other end. Then twist that end around both lines and through the loop. Do not pull it tight. Instead, continue to twist that same end through the loop four more times. Make sure that each new twist is not on top of an earlier twist; rather, each twist should be next to the earlier one so that all the twists are right against the original two lines. Then grab that end in one hand and the other line in the other hand and pull it tight. It will form a small cylindrical knot, and you should have at least 4 inches of the other end hanging out from it.

Next, tie the exact same knot using the other end. When you have finished, you should be left with two small, cylindrical knots about an inch apart. Grab the two lines on either side of those knots, and pull tight. The two small knots slide together to form one very strong knot that secures the two lines together. Trim this knot very closely so that almost no ends are visible. Doing this decreases the chance of your line getting caught on the knot.

Then, continue spooling on the new line. One caution: After you have cut off the old line, be certain that you replace your reel cover and that you run the new line back through the guides from the far end of the rod toward the reel before you tie this knot. This makes spooling the line (reeling in the line) much easier. If you do not, there will be no guides, your new line may tangle around itself, and you will be forced to provide a manual guide with your thumb and index finger, which is clumsy and hard on your skin. New line also leaves a thin film of white powder on your skin, which can cause dryness and cracking.

You can also use a single uni knot to tie the line to your spinner or swivel as well. Run the end of the line through the eyehole and back parallel to the main line. Then follow the directions above to create a single knot tight against the eyehole.

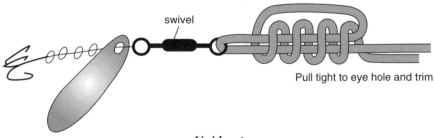

swivel

Pull tight to eye hole and trim

Uni knot

Thus you have three choices—the simple knot, the improved clinch knot, and the uni knot—to attach your spinner to the line. Choose whichever one you are most comfortable with. Further explanations of these knots and others can be found on-line at www.netknots.com/html/fishing_knots.html.

CHAPTER SIX

Stream Characteristics

STREAM TYPE

Two basic stream types exist—freestone streams and limestone streams. The difference is in the type of rock the stream flows over.

Freestone streams tend to be cleaner, clearer streams, because the rock over which they flow does not erode very quickly. Freestoners become cloudy or muddy only when it rains hard enough to cause soil erosion. I know some freestoners that remain clear even during heavy rains, because they flow directly over rock and have almost no soil to erode.

Limestone, in contrast, erodes very quickly, and limestone streams are usually marked by a cloudy, chalky color. Limestoners are often fed by large springs that keep water temperatures more stable during cold winters and warm summers. They also promote aquatic plant and insect growth, which provides a great deal of food for trout to eat. This means there are usually more trout per mile on a limestoner than on a freestoner of the same size. However, there are many more freestoners than limestoners in the United States.

The most important difference in fishing the two with spinners is the clarity of the water, rather than the water temperature, which is a bit more important with fly and natural bait fishing. Generally, freestoners are more conducive to spinner fishing because we tend to rely on vision more than our other senses when trout fishing. And seeing is believing.

Freestone Streams

Unlike the fly fisherman, who casts to feeding trout, the spin fisherman can usually attract any trout from any part of the hole at any given time. If a trout has not recently been disturbed, it rarely (less than 10 percent of the time) refuses to at least follow a spinner and see what it is. That's not the case with flies and natural bait, which trout often refuse.

In the relatively clear water of freestone streams, you can see when a trout is interested and where that trout was before you cast. You can also watch where that trout goes if you don't catch it on the first try, and then you can make a proper cast to it.

In clear freestoners, trout tend to hide themselves more quickly than in cloudy streams. They stick closer to any cover they can find, and that makes it doubly important to fish the cover closely. Although spinners can draw trout out from almost anywhere in a hole, you are much more likely to catch that trout if you put the lure close enough so the fish doesn't have time to think about it and doesn't have to move too far.

The problem with clear streams, especially in low-water conditions, is that you must approach with caution, which takes time. In addition, you have to be able to make long casts and thus long retrieves, which also takes time.

The three standard approaches to a clear stream are:

1. Fish directly upstream. A trout's vision is poorest to the rear.
2. Lower your height. The closer you are to the water level, the less chance there is that the trout will see you. This often means kneeling to cast and crawling on your hands and knees or even on your belly. Personally, I rarely crawl for any ordinary fish. It takes away valuable time that could be spent fishing in easier locations. But if I'm after a particularly large fish, I'll do whatever it takes.
3. Cast from well behind the bank. The farther you are from the stream, the less likely you are to scare the trout.

Limestone Streams

Approach usually isn't as much of an issue with limestone streams. Their cloudy waters allow you to approach with somewhat less caution and yet greater protection, because the fish can't see as well through the murk. That does two things: You spend less time making a less cautious approach, and it allows you to cast from wherever you choose.

But as much as the fish can't see you, you can't see the fish either. That creates the problem of where to cast and where to wade. Casting is relatively simple, because you fish the cover just as you would a clear stream, but with a little extra caution because you can't always see what's underneath the surface. Don't forget the rest of the hole, however. Trout are likely to be resting or feeding away from cover in a limestoner, so you should fish the entire hole. This means that fishing a limestoner generally takes more time than fishing a freestoner of the same size, because you have to cast into every likely spot. In a clear stream, I often pass by some good water after only one cast (just to be sure), because I can plainly see that there are no trout.

Lick Run, a limestone stream in Centre County, Pennsylvania, is a trophy trout water.

By the way, even if you aren't catching fish, don't be so sure that there are no trout unless you have some corroborating evidence. I once observed the Pennsylvania Fish Commission "shock fish" a stream—a procedure whereby they shock the water with electrodes to stun the fish, which then float to the surface, where they are counted and measured. I had already fished through that section of the stream and was certain that there were no more than a handful of trout, and no big ones. To my surprise, they fished out several dozen trout, including two better than 16 inches. And I've heard similar stories from other people.

You must also be careful where you wade in a limestoner. Feeding trout can often be found in the shallow water near the tail of a pool, and more than once I've scared trout by wading in without thinking. Don't make that mistake. As you're wading in, make a cast to the shallow water in front of you. You'll sometimes get a strike, and if you don't, at least you won't be kicking yourself for missing the chance.

Oddly, freestoners are the same as limestoners with regard to visibility when they become cloudy after a rain. When a normally clear stream becomes muddy, fish it as though it were a limestoner. In fact, trout act much the same way in a muddy freestoner as they do in a limestoner; however, they are sometimes more apt to bite. Some of my best days have been on muddy freestoners.

STREAM SIZE AND FLOW

Besides stream type, the other main stream variations are size and rate of flow. Small size can greatly increase your speed because you need fewer casts to cover a hole. Don't be fooled, however. Small streams frequently have more holes than large streams do, so it can take nearly as long to fish a mile on a small stream as on a large one. Although small streams have fewer trout, because there are more holes, the trout you find will not have been disturbed (at least not by you). In all but the largest streams, catching one trout often disturbs the entire hole.

Larger streams hold more fish and tend to hold them longer into the summer months. Plus, they hold more large fish, so if you're after the lunkers, fish the bigger water. But don't be surprised to catch a big one on a small stream. That 22-inch rainbow I mentioned earlier came from a stream less than 10 feet wide.

Larger streams also have a stronger flow, so you may want to use a heavier spinner or attach some weight to reach the bottom of the deep pools. Remember that a larger spinner creates more drag and is slower to retrieve, so compensate for that. If you attach weight, be sure that it is as close to the spinner as possible to provide an accurate cast.

Two streams of equal width can also be very different because of their flow rate. A swift stream requires a lure heavy enough to sink quickly and not be carried downstream, plus it requires a quick retrieval. Trout in swift current tend to strike quicker and harder than those in slow-moving streams—they have to, or else their food would be carried away. Be ready to set the hook at all times.

ADJUSTING RETRIEVES FOR STREAM CONSIDERATIONS

When facing upstream and retrieving the spinner downstream, a fast current often doesn't allow the spinner to spin as it needs to. This means you're not retrieving quickly enough. You must always pull the lure faster than the current, and in high water, that sometimes means reeling like a madman.

Trout in slow currents behave differently. They often take their time and cruise slowly behind a lure without taking it. On some streams, I've seen trout follow up to 15 feet behind the lure, yet they follow it nearly to my feet. It can be quite frustrating. The key in slow water is to drag the lure slowly by the trout (being too accurate and hitting trout on the retrieve often spooks them). Fast retrieves rarely work in slow water.

> *In general, retrieve a spinner fast in fast water and slow in slow water.*

Remember this tip: Retrieve fast in fast water and slow in slow water. Having said that, however, there are specific places where a slow retrieve is very effective—in both slow and fast water. For instance, when you're retrieving the spinner along a likely hiding place (a log, rock, or bank), there are usually small eddies in such spots, which is part of the reason the trout is there. In these likely trout holds, retrieve your lure as slowly as possible in the specific places you expect the trout to be. The goal is to keep it spinning in the water as long as possible before breaking the surface. Using this tactic, I've often caught trout just as I was about to pull the lure out of the water.

> *No matter what you do with your spinner in the water, make sure the blade is spinning.*

Whether in fast water or slow water, there is only one prerequisite to catching trout: The spinner has to spin. No matter what else I've said, make sure that thing is spinning.

CHAPTER SEVEN

The Weather

Weather is probably the most fickle element in trout fishing (next to the trout, of course). It can be totally unpredictable and cause considerable havoc if you don't know how to work with it effectively.

Three basic weather conditions confront all anglers—rain, normal weather, and drought. Of these, rainy conditions are the most complicated. The other weather-related factor is temperature. Don't assume that cold weather and rain, or hot weather and drought, go hand in hand, though. Obviously, there are a lot of combinations. Rain and drought affect water levels, and water levels affect how you fish. Temperatures affect when trout feed, which affects when and where you fish.

NORMAL CONDITIONS
Obviously, normal conditions are the simplest. Fish normally, as I've described in previous chapters.

DROUGHT
Dry weather is also relatively simple. Prolonged dry weather makes water levels drop, so the trout have to find better places to hide. They move to the deepest parts of the holes, hide beneath rocks and logs, and stick close to the banks. But because they can see you more easily, they also scare more easily. That makes your approach very important. Stay out of the water entirely whenever you can. Many fishermen creep up on holes very low to the ground, often crawling on their stomachs.

Casting distance is the most important factor in low-water stream fishing with spinners. You need to cast farther beyond the trout and stand back farther from it, or else risk scaring it off. It's a good idea to use lighter line (switch from 6- to 4-pound test), with the same size spinner as usual. This allows you to cast farther. The idea is to cast at least 5 feet beyond the trout and to stand several feet back from the water's edge (ideally, 10 feet or more) during low-water conditions.

RAIN

Wet, rainy weather is by far the most complicated but potentially the most rewarding. It makes finding the biting trout more difficult, but when you find them the fishing is usually better than normal.

The first problem with rain, obviously, is flooding. Never fish in a flood, and never try to cross a swollen stream. One false step could mean serious injury or even death. However, you generally don't have to go very far to find a fishable stream—usually within a 30-minute drive (see below).

The second problem with rain is that it doesn't fall in the same amounts everywhere. Rain may muddy one stream, but another one just a few miles away might still be low and clear. That's especially true in the case of thunderstorms. It's important to be aware of where the rain is. If you have The Weather Channel or Internet access to weather sites, you have a great resource, because

> *Never try to cross a flooding or swollen stream.*

they provide local radar pictures. Some sites, such as AccuWeather.com, even provide Doppler radar rainfall estimates for an entire state for the previous hour, 3 hours, 24 hours, and longer intervals.

Little Fishing Creek in Centre County, Pennsylvania, flooded its banks in 1992. It wasn't safe to fish here, but we did well on streams nearby.

The third problem with rain is simply that it represents a change, and you can never be sure how the trout will react to it. Usually, rain produces good fishing. Sometimes it makes the fishing spectacular, but at other times, the trout seem to disappear. Which will happen to you? Typically, it depends on the water temperature, discussed later. Here are some basic tactics for high-water fishing and beating the rain. The first three tips deal with knowing when to fish and where to go.

1. Have confidence. The trout are still there during high water, and you can catch them if you know how. Don't stay home because of rain. I often go fishing *because* it's raining.
2. Know where the rain is heaviest. If the rain is heavy and a flood is threatening, you want to get away from the heavy rain. If it's been dry for a month and the streams are low, however, you want to find the heavy rain.
3. As long as you can walk the bank safely, you can catch trout.

> Within a 30-minute drive of a flooded stream you can usually find one low enough to fish.

The next few tips deal with where the fish are in the stream and how to catch them.

4. When rain clouds a stream, you can approach without a great deal of caution, but you should still try to stay out of the water.
5. As long as the stream is not at or close to flood stage, trout are generally in their normal places. If anything, they may be feeding a little farther than normal. So fish normally.
6. When the water is very high but still within the banks, trout dive deeper in the pools and move behind rocks, logs, and anything else that slows the current. Concentrate on those places, and fish a little deeper in the big pools. Keep at least a $1/8$-ounce spinner on your line. Sometimes a heavier spinner is more effective.
7. When the water is right at flood stage but you can still walk the bank, trout often move to the eddies on the edge of the stream. (This is especially true of recently stocked trout.) Don't wade in those calm spots, or you'll probably wade right past the trout. Instead, stay on the bank and run your spinner slowly through those eddies, concentrating on any calm spot along a log or rock with room underneath for trout. When possible, but with safety in mind, cross the stream and fish the opposite bank, where other fishermen usually don't go. That's a good way to be the first to cast for a bunch of trout hiding in the eddies during high water. Be aware, however, that trout move quickly away from the banks and back into fairly normal positions long before the stream returns to normal.

WATER TEMPERATURE

Though not as important to spinning as it is to fly fishing, water temperature is still a significant factor. A stream thermometer can help guide you, especially when you're fishing outside of the typical spring months.

It is now well known and accepted that trout feed best when water temperatures are in the mid-50s through the mid-60s. Trout take in oxygen better when temperatures are in this range. Brook trout tend to feed better in slightly cooler temperatures than do rainbow and brown trout, but in general, the closer to 60 degrees the water is, the more likely you are to find feeding trout. Other factors play a role, however, which is why temperature itself is no guarantee. When water temperatures soar into the upper 70s and 80s, many trout die. This occurs in some of the flat streams up the East Coast into southern New England, but most streams in the Appalachian and Rocky Mountains have water temperatures within tolerable limits.

Although knowing the stream temperature is helpful, you can't predict with certainty how willing the trout will be to take your spinner. Here are some tips:

1. Buy a water thermometer and take readings every day.
2. As long as the water temperature is within the limits noted, you can be sure that temperature is not the reason why the trout aren't biting.
3. If the water temperature remains the same for an extended period—even at the optimal temperature—expect the fishing to be average for that temperature range.
4. If the water temperature suddenly changes toward the optimal feeding temperature (usually this means cooling due to rain), expect fishing to improve.
5. If the water temperature has consistently been well below the lower limit (or above the upper limit), expect trout to feed when the temperature rises (or falls) even a few degrees—even if it never gets within the limits noted.
6. During both cool conditions and warm conditions outside the limits, expect the trout to be sluggish or lethargic due to a lack of oxygen. This means that you should use a much slower retrieve in most cases.
7. During warm weather especially, look for spring-fed streams (limestone streams are the best bets). Cool spring waters help keep stream temperatures within the trout's feeding range. In particular, concentrate your fishing downstream from the spring itself. In warm weather, trout have a tendency to gather at or below a spring.

RAINFALL PLUS TEMPERATURE

When you combine both factors—precipitation and temperature—you find that normal weather conditions lead to average fishing, in general. Changes in the weather produce the best opportunities, especially a cool rain shower after a warm spell. The combination of cloudy water, more food being carried in the stream, and temperatures in the optimal feeding range brings the fish out to feed. Any change in temperature toward the optimal, combined with any water level, should provide good fishing. Use this basic knowledge to your advantage. Avoid fishing only in the worst weather conditions, and plan your outings around the weather.

Let's say it's been 90 degrees almost all week, and a rain-bearing cold front is due early Sunday morning. If you have a choice between fishing on Saturday or Sunday, you would be a lunatic to choose Saturday. Sunday is the better choice, especially the first hour after the rain ends.

Factoring in the weather isn't difficult, but you must pay attention to it. It can make a big difference in how much you enjoy your outing.

ELECTRICAL STORMS

Never fish during a lightning storm. Lightning kills more people than any other act of nature. In fact, the vast majority of victims are men pursuing recreational activities on summer afternoons. Your home, cabin, or car is the safest place. If you're caught away from those places, don't take shelter under trees. Find the lowest spot you can, minimize your contact with the ground, and keep your rod down and out of your hands altogether.

> *Never fish during a lightning storm. Lightning kills more people than any other act of nature. The vast majority of lightning strike victims are men pursuing recreational activities on summer afternoons.*

CHAPTER EIGHT

Late-Season Spinning

Only minor adjustments need to be made in each season. But with these few changes, summer and autumn in particular can be excellent times to fish. Autumn provides the right temperatures and an almost complete lack of fishing pressure (necessary to catch trout in the eastern United States). Plus the scenery is spectacular.

SUMMER

The most important factor in summer fishing is the temperature. Even regions cool enough to support trout over the summer may not be cool enough to keep them feeding consistently. Using the guidelines from chapter 7, measure the temperatures of the streams you generally fish to see if they're within the trout's range. If they're not, don't bother fishing those streams for trout, because you'll just be wasting your time. If the streams around you are too warm, take a drive to cooler climes.

Once you reach the stream, you'll find a few changes in the trout's habits. First, morning and evening are clearly the best times to fish spinners in the summer, because temperatures are usually in the feeding range then. Since the water level is usually lower due to a lack of rainfall, trout are very wary or spooky. You rarely find trout sitting in the middle of the stream, which they often do in the spring. They tend to hide even more than usual under rocks, logs, and banks.

Since the water is so low and the fish so spooky, any splash too near their hiding place can frighten the trout, and they won't feed. Therefore, you need to cast far beyond where you think the trout are. That's why I recommend keeping a heavier spinner on your line and perhaps using a lighter line, because you can cast farther with that combination.

A trout can also see and hear you much better in low water. It is usually advisable to fish upstream, because trout can't see as well behind themselves. If you have to approach from the sides or from above, keep a very low profile. Also on your approach, stop a few feet short of where you would normally stand and make a longer cast. If you don't, you'll scare a lot of trout.

In the summer, trout tend to take as little time as possible to catch their food. Expect them to fire out sharply from their hiding places and then turn and run back immediately after hitting your spinner. It may be the most exciting time to catch trout because of their sheer power and quickness.

Also because the water is low, you don't have as much room under the water for your spinner. You're more likely to get caught on bottom stones during the summer. The best way to counter this is to reel a little more quickly (the trout usually move more quickly too) and keep your rod tip up higher. That allows you to keep it spinning even in 2 or 3 inches of water, and believe me, the trout will chase it there. When a trout does chase it that far, it is important that you don't get stuck on a rock. It's better to pull the spinner out from under the trout's nose than to get caught and be forced to wade in and remove it, which will surely ruin the hole.

Of utmost importance in the summer (and fall) is whether the stretch has been fished ahead of you. Since the trout are so spooky, another fisherman fishing ahead of you can be devastating. He will likely scare all the fish in a stretch, leaving you without a chance.

Although low, warm summer waters provide perhaps the poorest fishing of the year next to winter, water levels aren't always low in the summer. Often a thunderstorm or simply a heavy rain raises the water level. These can be spectacular fishing times, since the trout that were not feeding freely in low water are now out in search of food. Rain also cools the water and helps keep the temperature in the feeding range. If you have a choice between fishing before or after a summer rain, always choose after.

> *In the summer, more than any other time, avoid fishing behind someone else— especially if that person is fishing spinners.*

In high-water summer conditions, expect the trout to be out in the middle of the stream feeding. You should still fish near the rocks, logs, and banks, but the trout are likely to be a short distance from them. If the water is muddy enough that you can't see the fish, you can approach and cast any way you like. When the summer waters are high, fish much as you would during the spring.

AUTUMN

In contrast to summer, in autumn, trout are rarely found hiding. Few fishermen do much fishing in the fall, which means that the trout don't need

A gorgeous autumn afternoon on a lightly fished section of Black Moshannon Creek in Centre County, Pennsylvania. In some states, such as Pennsylvania, fall stocking programs on sections of some popular streams give anglers additional access to stocked trout.

to hide and can feed freely. However, don't expect them to be exactly where they were in the spring. When trout haven't been bothered, they like to feed in shallow water. In the spring, you find them in the deep water because of the fishing pressure, but in the fall, trout move to the tails or heads of the holes to feed and to spawn.

The biggest change here is your approach. Be aware that trout will be sitting almost into the riffles at the bottom of a calm hole (especially in sunny holes). This means that you should stop well short of the hole and make a cast to the tail itself. You'll be surprised how often trout lie there—even large trout.

> *In the fall, trout often sit almost in the riffles at the bottom of a hole.*

The water is often shallow in the fall, and that can create problems with snagging fallen leaves. Though pretty, leaves can be annoying, especially when the wind is blowing them from the trees. Otherwise, you simply have to be more careful about keeping your spinner off the bottom.

Trout do not bite as aggressively during the fall as they do in the summer or even the spring. They often put their mouths around a spinner and simply hold there instead of turning to run, as they do at other times. They are often listless and don't put up a very good fight. Much of this is due to spawning, which tires the trout somewhat. For this reason, it is important to locate a trout, place a cast beyond it, and reel the lure as close as you can to its nose. The trout will often take the spinner if it doesn't have to do more than open its mouth or turn its head, as opposed to the summer, when such a close cast would scare it away.

Be aware that many states have limits on the amount of fish you can kill, and some streams may be off limits in the fall. Check your state's regulations to be sure the stream you want to fish is open.

Please do not disturb any trout you see spawning. When trout spawn they can usually be found finning in very shallow water and sweeping out gravel beds with their tails. It is important that these areas not be disturbed so the trout can reproduce. Many noted anglers have called for a ban on fall trout fishing, because they fear that we are disturbing these nests. Autumn trout fishing is some of the best, yet I advise you to keep your distance from any spawning beds you find.

> *Do not disturb any trout you see spawning. It might kill them.*

WINTER

Winter's the best time to get out your magazines and catalogs, because trout don't bite in the winter, right? Wrong. Last year, I caught trout

An ice storm blanketed Ridley Creek in Delaware County, Pennsylvania, just west of Philadelphia, in 1994. Despite the slippery conditions on land, wading in the stream produced several hungry trout. While some states close most streams to fishing in the fall and winter until opening day in the spring, others regulate some streams and sections differently to provide year-round angling opportunities.

Casting a line on a warm winter day

during every month. Many fishermen do. Trout don't hibernate, so they still need to eat. But because they're cold-blooded, their metabolism slows down in cold weather. As a result, they don't eat as much during the winter, which means that you won't catch as many, even with spinners.

> *Trout do not hibernate, so they still need to eat, even in winter.*

Once again, water temperature is important. Use the guidelines in chapter 7 to measure your favorite trout streams and determine whether they're within the limits. If you know of any spring-fed waters (specifically limestone-fed streams), they are good bets. Springs provide warmer water during the winter, and trout are often found feeding below springs. Since a trout's metabolism is slower in the winter, the fish tends to move slower. This means that your retrieve must be slower as well. Winter trout tend to go deep into the hole, because the surface is chilled by the colder air above (and may even be frozen). Use a slow, deep, trolling retrieve to get the best results in winter. Since the trout are usually deep, your approach is not terribly important. Also, expect very little competition in the winter. Most fishermen (including myself) believe that fishing is a warm-weather sport.

Afterword:
Motivation and Timing

You may be thinking, "Wow, there really isn't much to this." If this is an attitude you've acquired by reading this book, it was definitely worth reading. Even if you only picked up a few tips that will increase your enjoyment, it was worth it. Once you realize how simple spinner fishing can be, you won't waste a lot of time and effort on the wrong equipment, methods, or approaches. That's good.

The bad part is that reading isn't doing. You've got to get out there and fish to get a feel for what I've said. There are a lot of subtleties that are almost impossible to explain, so I haven't tried. Learning those subtleties is part of the fun of fishing.

I almost wish you hadn't read this book, because if you take my advice to heart, you might take away some of my trout! But if you're serious about wanting to catch more fish, motivation and timing are absolutely vital. The first is vital to any fisherman, and the second is especially vital to a spinner fisherman.

> **Be motivated. Take the initiative and get up early. Start catching fish at dawn. You can sleep in the afternoon, when everyone else is fishing.**

I don't care what time of year it is, you can't catch trout if you're sitting at home. Most of you want to catch more trout, but you can't seem to get off your couches to do it; or when you do, it's only for a few hours on Sunday afternoon—the worst time to go spinner fishing, after everyone and his brother have had a crack at your trout.

Be motivated. Take the initiative to get up early—earlier than me—and start catching trout at dawn. You can take a nap in the afternoon when everyone else is out fishing. You'll face less competition, catch more trout, get the same amount of sleep, and be more successful.

Take your fishing clothes to work and stop by the stream in the evening. Convince yourself to get up very early and catch a few before

Alongside several fly fishermen on a tremendous autumn afternoon. Fall foliage on the First Fork of Sinnemahoning Creek in Potter County, Pennsylvania, is a delightful bonus to the beauty of fall trout fishing.

work. If you have a choice, schedule your work on the weekends and fish the weekdays, when there's less competition.

If you're really serious, schedule a half or full vacation day for midweek or for the Friday (and maybe Thursday) prior to a fishing weekend. My father and his buddy generally go from Thursday through Saturday (sometimes Wednesday through Sunday) nearly every week during the stocking season.

What I'm saying is go as often as you can, stay as far away from other fishermen as you can, and keep moving if you want to catch trout. Getting the jump on the competition and fishing where and when no one else goes is what make a good spinner fisherman. Sure, you'll likely catch some trout

These two beauties came from out-of-the-way Mix Run in Cameron/Elk Counties of Pennsylvania. It's great to fool two big trout on a spinner on back-to-back casts!

> *Go as often as you can, keep moving, and stay far away from other fishermen if you want to catch trout.*

regardless of when you go, but the very successful spinner fisherman gets up earlier, fishes faster, and fishes farther than his competition. If there is a secret, now you know it.